a
thought
for
each day
in
1966

D. C. THOMSON & CO., LTD.
LONDON · GLASGOW · MANCHESTER · DUNDEE

The
FRIENDSHIP
BOOK
of
FRANCIS GAY

O Lord !   Thou knowest how busy
    I must be this day :
if I forget Thee, do not Thou forget me.

Prayer before the Battle of Edgehill
by Sir Philip Warwick.

SENTRY - GO

When folk come up to chat to me
Jock turns a watchful eye.
They never pass when he says " Halt !"
Boy !   They'd be daft to try.

.DAVID HOPE

HIGHLAND BURN

Strange how soon forgotten are the tiresome things in life,
When beauty fills the world with gladness, hiding all the strife.
As spring returns to bless us with a tumbling Highland stream,
The harshness of the winter fades and passes like a dream.

DAVID HOPE

JANUARY

I HAVE never been one who has laid great stress on New Year resolutions.

True, no harm whatever can be done by beginning a new year with a new determination to get rid of something unworthy and to make a real effort to fulfil any vow we may have vowed.

But you and I are frail children of dust, and with all the goodwill in the world we are likely to discover long before March that we are back again very much where we started.

But I do believe you and I can be better men or women if we begin every day with a little prayer that God will forgive us for what we have done wrong and bless us in all we try to do right.

Because I am not a saint, I find one step is enough for me and I must live a day at a time.

I rather think that gallant Englishman, Sir Francis Drake, knew that it is easier to promise to do a thing than to do it, and keep on doing it. At any rate, at this season, it may be worth our while making his famous prayer our own—

O Lord, when thou givest to thy servants to endeavour any great matter, grant us also to know that it is not the beginning, but the continuing of the same till it be thoroughly finished, which yieldeth the true glory. May every happiness be yours in the year that lies ahead.

GRACE and peace be multiplied unto you through the knowledge of God, and of Jesus our Lord.

MONDAY—JANUARY 3.

TOWARDS evening, a young man of eighteen makes his way to church. He is wearing the uniform of a Rover Scout.

The church is empty. The young man opens the door and enters the silent building. He goes to a pew and bows his head in prayer. Then he waits in the quietness, thinking about himself and his life.

For half an hour he does not move. Finally, after bowing his head once again, he rises and goes out into the evening sun, his solemn vigil over.

Every boy who wishes to become a Rover Scout must first spend this time of meditation in an empty church. It is called simply "The Vigil," and its purpose is to give the boys a chance to decide how they can become good men, and to think upon the vows they are about to make to God, their country, their family, and their friends.

I am sure none of these boys can come away from church without being the better for it.

TUESDAY—JANUARY 4.

IF any man's faith is founded on a rock it is that of the Rev. Alexander Caseby.

Every night, when most of the windows in his parish are dark, the lamp in Mr Caseby's study still burns. For he has divided his roll of members into seven parts, and before he goes to bed, he prays for a seventh of his congregation each night of the week.

He remembers them by name, speaks quietly to God of their special needs, and asks Him to bless them. In this way, every member of his flock is brought before their Maker every week.

I thank him, for in his humble walk with God he has brought blessing to a multitude.

WEDNESDAY—JANUARY 5.

HERE'S wishing you both health and wealth throughout the coming year,
With friends and fun, a kindly sun and lots and lots of cheer.
But most of all I hope you'll vow, in spite of good or ill,
However kind you've been—this year you will be kinder still!

THURSDAY—JANUARY 6.

FROM Canada comes a sweet little note from one of my girl friends there.

She is ninety, as lively as can be. One sentence in her latest letter has been with me ever since I read it—

" Oh, and just in case you ever feel a bit down-hearted, Francis, remember what George Macdonald says—' *God only knows how happy He could make us if only we would let Him.*' "

Surely that's a sermon in itself?

FRIDAY—JANUARY 7.

THE Lady of the House had a special idea some years ago. Whether or not it is wise, I am not sure, but it springs from a warm heart and very good intentions. Her argument is simply this— Almost everybody is remembered by somebody at Christmas or New Year. That's fine! But then come the chilly days afterwards—the excitement over . . . and quite a few lonely old people sitting by the fire with nothing but memories.

How wonderful to take some of them by happy surprise, and drop them a line or send them a little unexpected present in January! How nice, just when you think you are forgotten, to be remembered.

SATURDAY—JANUARY 8.

ON a cold winter's day nearly 100 years ago, a young woman lay in her parents' home in London, weary and restless after a long and trying illness. Her name was Kate Hankey, and so sorely had the illness drained her strength that she could hardly find words even to pray for help.

So she took up pen and paper, and in simple sentences, she wrote of her deep need. When she had finished, in front of her lay the lines that have become one of our best loved hymns—

　Tell me the old, old story
　　Of unseen things above,
　　Of Jesus and His glory,
　　Of Jesus and His love . . .

In every verse the old, old story speaks to us again, and it has never failed to bring boundless riches to all who have put their trust in it.

SUNDAY—JANUARY 9.

AS ye would that men should do to you, do ye also to them likewise.

MONDAY—JANUARY 10.

CLIMATE makes a vast difference to a country —and your own particular climate makes a vast difference to you.

What happens has a lot to do with the climate you take around with you. The mean person who is cold and chilly creates a climate which blights other folk.

But if only you carry about with you a warmth of feeling and kindliness you will meet charming people and somehow drop in for all sorts of happy little surprises which never come the way of churlish folk . . . because their climate is not right.

TUESDAY—JANUARY 11.

HARRY CHALK was an insurance man with a happy family and assured future.

Enough for most men—but Harry wasn't satisfied. Not, I hasten to add, because he wasn't getting enough from life, but because he felt he wasn't giving enough back in return. For his work took him into all kinds of homes and he saw that many people desperately needed help and faith. So he talked things over with his wife, and they decided to give up everything and serve others by joining the Mission to Deep-Sea Fishermen.

It was a big step, but in their hearts they knew their decision was right. Then, on the eve of taking up the new work, their baby son died.

Harry knew that on that night his whole future lay in the balance. If he had broken down then and begun to question the purpose of the God to whose service he was about to devote his life, he could not have gone on.

So, though their hearts were breaking, Harry and his wife knelt and asked their Maker to give them guidance and understanding—and when morning came they knew He had not failed them.

Now Harry is assistant superintendent of the Fishermen's Mission in Aberdeen and he's finding a challenge and fullness of life that surpasses anything he has ever known.

WEDNESDAY—JANUARY 12.

*H*OWEVER *hard and rough the road*
  You have to plod along ;
However lonely you may feel . . .
  Too sad to sing a song.
Keep on ! Who knows but that one day
  You'll stride a sunny, happy way ?

THURSDAY—JANUARY 13.

ONE of America's greatest humorists is Sam Levenson. One evening, at a party, somebody said he had been lucky as a child, and Sam said, "That goes for me, too—I was lucky as a child."

The remark caused laughter, because everybody knew that Sam came from the poorest of the poor.

But when the laughter had died down, Sam made it quite plain he was speaking the truth, and that he had not tried to be witty. "We were poor," he declared. "Nobody here knows *how* poor. But in spite of it, I was also rich and very happy —happy even when hungry because we were all hungry together, and I was much loved."

FRIDAY—JANUARY 14.

IN Glasgow there are 250 members of the Veteran Sea-Farers' Association. Many of them, after spending all their lives at sea, are now housebound or bedridden. All of them know that, at some time, they may need help. And when that does happen, all they do is send out their S O S.

You see, when each old sailor joins the Association, he is given a stamped postcard. It is addressed to the Association with their own name and address on the back. If help is needed urgently, the old sailor just drops the card into the nearest post-box.

It's better than a red flare or a morse message —for when it arrives, Mr Cowieson, secretary of the Association, drops whatever he's doing and sets off to answer the S O S.

Of course, he arrives in his car—not a lifeboat. And he doesn't bring lifebelts, but a warm smile and friendly advice. Yet who can doubt that this simple S O S does shield these old sailors from rock and tempest, and protect them wheresoe'er they go . . .?

SATURDAY—JANUARY 15.

ON Thursday evenings Miss Bessie May of Peterhead, makes her way to the prison.

You see, she trains the choir of the prison chapel, and every Thursday she practises with the prisoners for next Sunday's service. And how they love it !

Miss May doesn't know, nor does she care, what crime has brought them to Peterhead, and her trust in them is amply repaid, for always they are perfect gentlemen in her presence.

Hymns and prison may seem an unlikely mixture. But there's nothing strange about it to Miss May—or the prisoners of Peterhead.

SUNDAY—JANUARY 16.

BEHOLD, God is my salvation.

MONDAY—JANUARY 17.

I LIKE Moira, a pretty theatre nurse in a hospital. She works hard and long. You never hear her grumble—but when, at last, she gets some time off, she hurries home by bus to join her mother.

The minute Moira walks in she says, " Hello ! Sit down, Mum. Here's Nurse Moira on duty !"

From then on she's in charge—cleaning, tidying up, beginning and ending a week's baking—and seeing to Grandad, who is suffering from an incurable disease, and keeping a watchful eye on Grannie, whose memory is slipping and who'd be out of the house if she had half a chance.

That's Moira's little holiday at home. And she shoulders all that responsibility and sings as she lends a hand . . . all to give Mum a rest !

Is it surprising that I like Moira ?

TUESDAY—JANUARY 18.

"THE ABSENTEE'S ALPHABET" begins—
"I'd like to go to church but . . ."

A is for Auntie, who will come to tea,
B is for bed, which won't release me.
C is for car—" we need the fresh air "—
D is for dinner that Mum must prepare.
E is for enthusiasm, which I haven't got,
F is for foursome, which golfs quite a lot.
G is for garden, much " nearer God's heart,"
H is for husband, who won't play his part.
I for intruders who sit in my pew,
J for the jealousy shown by a few.
K is for knitting, which Mum likes so much,
L the old language, it's so out of touch.
M is for money, they always want more,
N for new tunes that I've not heard before.
O is for overtime, double on Sunday,
P the preparing I must do for Monday.
Q for queer noises which come from the choir,
R for the rector, he ought to retire.
S is for sermons, as dull as can be,
T for the telly I really must see.
U for unfriendliness I always find,
V for the voice of the woman behind.
W for weather, too much rain or snow,
X is for extras, too busy to go.
Y for young rowdies who sit at the back,
Z is for zeal—and that's just what I lack.

WEDNESDAY—JANUARY 19.

WASHING done, ironing done, all neatly stored
  away,
House looks neat, baby's sweet—he cut a tooth today !
Footsteps coming up the path, Daddy turns the key,
Joy's complete, life's a treat — Lucky, Lucky Me !

THE FRIENDSHIP BOOK

I LUNCHED one day with a successful business man.

One thing he had to say I shall not easily forget—
" You know, Mr Gay, it wasn't till I'd been married
five or six years that I realised, with a shock, that
the meanest thing a husband in business can do
is to go home every day with a load of grumbles.
I used to do so. Mary took it magnificently. She
sympathised. She was great.

" And then, one evening, it suddenly occurred to
me that I was never sharing with her the little
triumphs or the day's humour. I vowed there and
then to change my tactics, and ever since then I've
tried to take home to Mary at least one bit of good
news five days a week! "

There is something in it, isn't there?

IF you stepped into the churchyard at Coupar
Angus, and paused by a grave near the door,
you would see what is perhaps a unique memorial.

On the grave, set into a granite block, is a beauti-
fully polished copper casket filled with flowers,
flowers that never fade.

They were delicately made in enamelled wrought-
iron by Davie McPherson, a retired blacksmith, for
the grave of his wife.

Davie's wife loved flowers, but she never saw the
flowers he fashioned, for it was only after she died
that he began to make them. Often, he wished she
could have seen them—and that is why he made
this special casket of her favourite flowers.

You might argue that no artificial flowers, however skilfully made, can be so lovely as real ones.

But not the flowers that Davie made for his wife.
For each is fragrant with precious memories. . . .

THE FRIENDSHIP BOOK

A NEW road bridge is being built on the River Tay, linking Dundee and the north with Fife.

How are they managing to build it so straight and true? Of course, they have the help of scientific instruments, but, I'm told these would be useless without the two white marks. They're painted on a window-sill three floors up, just opposite the end of the bridge.

The builders, even when far out in the river, can see the marks on the high window-sill, and take their bearings from them, just as, in olden days, sailors took their bearings from the Pole Star.

It's a bit like life, isn't it? For how much we all need something to look up to if we're to make anything fine of ourselves!

THOU shalt love the Lord thy God with all thy heart.

NOT long ago an old lady lay dying. Her neighbour, a widow, sat with her.

The door opened and the neighbour's daughter, a girl of 11, came quietly in. She tiptoed to the bedside and stood looking down, heartbroken.

Then, sensing someone there, the old woman opened her eyes and looked up at the weeping girl. " Lassie," she whispered, " don't cry for me. I've as many friends on the other side as I have here."

You see, " there " was as real to her as " here," and she was ready to go forward, with boundless trust, to meet her friends and her Maker.

It is when we hear of experiences like this that we understand the meaning of true faith.

THE FRIENDSHIP BOOK

I HAVE attended a child's funeral only three or four times.

Such services are always deeply moving, and the one at which I was present recently was no exception.

We were a small company—father and mother, a few relatives and only a handful of friends, among them the father's employer. Perhaps it was because we were so few that the church seemed so big and so chilly that grey afternoon.

That the stricken parents should weep was to be expected. That relatives and intimate friends should weep was not surprising. But what did surprise me was the face of my friend's employer.

He is a big man with grey hair and lined cheeks. Everybody knows he can drive a hard bargain and implement hard decisions. Yet there he sat, quite unashamed as tears trickled down his face.

When the little service was over I came out of the kirk with a tumult in mind and heart—sorrow and sympathy for the bereaved parents, a sense of personal loss and a disturbing awareness that you never really know any other living soul. For 30 years I have imagined I knew that grey-haired business man. But I had suddenly discovered I did not know him at all.

" WELL, after all," I said to her,
    " A cat is but a cat.
Poor Tibbs is gone, but surely you've
    No need to weep at that !"
" How strange," sighed she, " it's going to be
    So different from before,
To have no one at all to do
    A bit of something for !"

THE FRIENDSHIP BOOK

JIMMY BOYD lives in a cottage in the hills, with a garden at the front and seven hives of bees at the back. He's been looking after the Galashiels to Selkirk road for over twenty years with a pride and faithfulness that would shame many a man.

For one thing, Jimmy never wastes time. If it takes him 20 minutes to sit down by the roadside and eat his mid-day piece, then he stops for 20 minutes and no more.

In winter, when you and I are safe and warm in bed, Jimmy often rises in the small hours, wraps himself in his thickest coat, pulls out his stoutest boots, and strikes out into a blizzard to be sure the road is safe for the milk lorries or the first bus. And he does it all with a cheerfulness that warms the heart.

Aye, Jimmy may be a humble man in a humble job—but he and his like are the salt of the earth.

A FRIEND received a letter from Canada and written on the envelope was this verse:——
Dear letter, go upon your way
 O'er mountain, plain, and sea;
God bless all those who speed your flight
 To where I wish you now to be.
And bless all those beneath the roof
 Where I would bid you rest,
And bless ev'n more the one to whom
 This letter is addressed.

A nice idea—and it made me wonder how many hearts the letter had warmed on its way from Canada —the posties who collected and delivered it, the men in the sorting office—aye, and all the folk (including you and me), who heard about it !

SATURDAY—JANUARY 29.

I OVERTOOK William Thomson a minute before he reached his garden gate late one afternoon. It was easy overtaking the old gentleman — he is not too nimble. "What are you doing out?" I demanded. "Mrs Thomson told me you were on the sick list."

"And I was," said he. "But not all that ill, you know. I really did want to change my library book, so I toddled off this afternoon—but I'm afraid I delayed awhile. It's rather later than I intended . . ."

I shook my head. I opened his gate, and said— "You ought to have more sense. You'd only to ask me or my wife, and we could have changed the library book for you."

Mr Thomson inclined his head. He smiled graciously, but there was a hint of pride in his voice as he said—"I know. I know—and it's kind of you. But you see, I was brought up on the principle that you never, never ask help of anybody if you can possibly do it yourself."

It was graciously said, as I have remarked. And I shall long remember it. How gloriously independent folk used to be! I wonder if in these days . . .

SUNDAY—JANUARY 30.

THE Son of man is come to seek and to save that which was lost.

MONDAY—JANUARY 31.

THE angler is in danger of losing his reputation as the world's best line-shooter. A motorist, defending himself in court on a charge of speeding said : "I was only going at walking pace, sir. No more than twenty miles an hour!"

FEBRUARY

THIS poem is dedicated to "The Night Nurse,"
and signed simply "By a patient in Ward 16."
I cannot tell you which hospital it was written in
but I feel it says everything that we all feel for these
splendid girls who do so much to ease the burden of
others :—

> She keeps her lonely vigil through the dark
>   and dreary night,
> Alert and silent, watching in the dimly burning
>   light.
> Her presence is a blessing, for she's ready to
>   perform
> The little tasks that make her patient comfy,
>   safe and warm.
> Kind, sensible and able, and quiet as a mouse,
> She brings a sense of comfort to the troubled
>   in the house;
> For they can go to sleep at night, and know
>   that she is there,
> Content to leave their loved ones to her wise
>   and tender care.
> God be with such good women as they watch
>   the long night through,
> And may they be rewarded for the splendid
>   work they do.

> *FROM my small window, looking out,*
>   *I see not only rain and snow*
> *Lashed by the howling gales, but fields*
>   *Where smiling springtime flowers blow;*
> *And though these days are chill and dark,*
>   *I listen to the singing lark !*

THE FRIENDSHIP BOOK

THURSDAY—FEBRUARY 3.

A LIVELY, attractive spinster I know is back at the office after being off with what she calls a spell of nerves.

I am glad to say she is looking as smart and happy as usual. But I think she has had a bad time.

" I just went to pieces," she admitted. " For the first time in my life I was sorry for myself, and I just couldn't stop thinking about me! If I buttered some toast, I wondered why I put so much or so little butter on. I couldn't go out without trying to fathom why I hadn't stayed at home—and if I stayed indoors I began searching my mind to find out just why I didn't want to go out . . . "

Then, smiling bravely, she said, " My advice to folk with nerves is—It's dangerous to look in too much. So look out !"

Rather witty, I think—and also profound.

FRIDAY—FEBRUARY 4.

SOME years ago he was one of the most widely-known and most highly respected of all American financiers.

He was immensely wealthy, a wizard with figures, and even his whisper could bring about rises and falls on the New York Stock Exchange. He was almost as powerful as the President.

But he overreached himself and went from the court, chained to a negro, to the cells, where his fame fell from him. He found himself nobody—merely a prisoner with a number.

One day a minister looked into his cell. The financier was sitting cross-legged. He held a ball of twine and a needle and was making bags.

" Hello," said the minister. " Sewing?"

" No," was the reply. " Reaping."

SATURDAY—FEBRUARY 5.

SO live this day that at the end you may be ashamed of nothing and glad of something you have done, or have tried to do.

So live this day that at the end someone may bless you for what you have done or have tried to do.

So live this day that at the end you may with a clear conscience look up to God, who knows all you have done or have tried to do . . .

SUNDAY—FEBRUARY 6.

THE Lord make you to increase and abound in love one toward another, and toward all men.

MONDAY—FEBRUARY 7.

I DOUBT if you have ever heard of old John Hughes of the Rhondda Valley.

At 12 John left school and went to work as a doorboy at a colliery. Later he became a railwayman, and there he remained, humble and contented, until he died in 1932, 59 years old.

Why am I telling you all this? Well, all his life, like many Welshmen, John loved singing. It was he who composed the wonderful tune which he called " Cwm Rhondda "—Welsh for " The Rhondda Valley "—for, he thought, what better name could he give it than that of the place that had been his home all his life?

We sing it still to the great Welsh hymn for which it was composed, "Guide Me, O Thou Great Jehovah." And who among us can keep his heart from lifting at the glorious, soaring chorus that was a humble railwayman's gift to the world?

Strong Deliverer, strong Deliverer,
Be Thou still my strength and shield . . .

TEA TIME

A very handsome teapot, not a doubt.
Aristocratic!   What a noble curving spout!
But I ask you!   Is it better at its job
Than the little old brown pot upon my hob?

DAVID HOPE

ENCHANTMENT

I dreamed a dream by the lonely strand,
And in it I saw an enchanted land
Where every man was good and true,
And I wished I could make my life anew.
I swore that day my ways to mend,
Till every man should be my friend . . .

DAVID HOPE

THE FRIENDSHIP BOOK

AS a fine man was laid to rest in the cemetery at Loanhead, 30 London bobbies, all in their best uniforms, stepped forward one by one to the foot of the grave. There they stood to attention and saluted. Then, after pausing for a moment, they wheeled to the right and marched back to their places at the graveside.

Who, you ask, was the man they were honouring in this way? He was David Wilson, a Loanhead man who, in 1939, left his native town to join the Metropolitan Police in London.

His beat was not an easy one, but the tall, burly bobby with the Scots voice soon won his way into the hearts of the folk who lived there. And in the years that were to come, they found in Dave Wilson a faithful friend. For, believe me, what he did for them went far beyond the call of duty. There was the pensioner in a condemned tenement, for whom he found a new house . . . the old folk on his beat whose messages he did, and whose guardian he was . . . and there were many, many more he helped.

That is why there were more flowers and wreaths at Dave's funeral than Loanhead had ever seen before. And that is why the 30 bobbies came all the way from London to pay their tribute.

I add my own tribute now, for all that he was, and all that he did.

DEAR Lord, please hear my little prayer
For all who suffer pain;
And, if it be Thy will, grant, Lord,
They may be well again.
And bless all those who, loving, long
To see their dear ones well and strong.

THURSDAY—FEBRUARY 10.

UP on the bleak hillside, alone in the winter darkness, stands the little old church.

Only a few folk turn out from their firesides, bend before the wind, and toil up the road, and most of them are white-haired. They sing a hymn or two; they bow as the minister prays for them and for all the wide world; they listen to the sermon . . .

When you think that for every one who attended that Sunday evening service, hundreds within a few miles of the church did not attend and never even thought of it, why not let the preaching and singing and praying drop out of use altogether?

But however carelessly men and women live today, the truth still needs to be preached, hearts still need to be warmed by singing the great hymns which stirred earlier generations, prayers are still needed, perhaps more than ever, for those who have no time for religion. And the church on the hill needs still to light its windows that men and women may find their way back to God.

FRIDAY—FEBRUARY 11.

A FRIEND was telling us one day that she had been having a talk with her doctor.

It was about the bringing up of children. She asked—" When all is said and done, Doctor, what do you think is the most important factor if they are to grow up strong and happy and rightly adjusted for life?"

The medical man did not say good food or plenty of sleep or no end of exercise or firm discipline or doses of cod liver oil. He just smiled and said—" By far the most important thing is that they go to sleep tired and happy."

It sounds very simple. I think it's very true.

SATURDAY—FEBRUARY 12.

I LIKE the story of how, at one stage in the building of the biggest single span in the Forth Railway Bridge the engineers discovered that when the final girders were dropped into place there was a gap of an inch or so.

An inch or so is not much in a span of over 1700 feet, but it meant that the holes did not overlap and the bolts could not be put into place.

Nobody was worried, however—and I rather think this discrepancy was according to plan. All the constructors did was to wait till the sun came up, its beams warming the metal, which duly expanded—and when the holes came level the bolts were put in place, and the great arch was securely complete.

Astonishing what the sun can do silently. Amazing what a bit of friendliness can accomplish—warming sad or troubled hearts and giving despairing folk new strength to keep on.

SUNDAY—FEBRUARY 13.

THE grace of our Lord Jesus Christ be with you.

MONDAY—FEBRUARY 14.

FEW of us find life easy.

I expect most days bring you a challenge. You feel, perhaps, you just can't keep on going to work so early on winter mornings. You've been carrying a burden at home a long time, but now you are at the end of your tether and must let go. You've tried and tried again to conquer a bad habit, and all to no purpose . . .

Well, all I want to say to you is : You never fail if you never stop trying.

TUESDAY—FEBRUARY 15.

FOR quite a time I've been writing regularly to Mrs Harding who is in hospital. I have written her many letters—cheery ones telling her to keep smiling and not to lose hope. I had the impression my letters were quite passable, till the other day.

It was the day I visited Mrs Harding.

Her big news was that (unknown to me) she had that morning received a letter from the Lady of the House, whereupon she insisted on reading it to me.

Believe it or not, the Lady of the House gave no advice, never told her to be brave or have faith . . . all she did was cover four sides of note-paper with lively bits and pieces of news about herself and about me and about our neighbours—the trouble she'd had to choose a new hat ; her visit to the hairdresser, and so on.

" Oh," murmured an enraptured Mrs Harding, " it's just the sort of letter I love—lots of news, no end of bits and pieces to chuckle over, just the things to make me want to get back home and take up life where I put it down !"

I raise my hat to the Lady of the House . . . she writes as she talks !

WEDNESDAY—FEBRUARY 16.

IF any little word of mine
Can make a heart the lighter,
If any little song of mine
Can make a heart the brighter,
God help me speak that little word,
And take my bit of singing,
And drop them in some lonely heart
To set its echoes ringing.

THE FRIENDSHIP BOOK

"I SHALL never forget that day," she told me. "It is several years since it happened, but it lives with me still. They were a poor old couple, but they had kept jogging along together, refusing charity, all in all to each other.

"Then she had cancer. Then—a year later—he had cancer. As a neighbour I went in every day. I did what I could. Life was misery for them—day after day becoming worse, sharing the same room.

"At last the doctor said both must go into hospital—he into the men's ward, she into the women's. It meant parting, knowing they would never see each other again.

"And I was there in the hour before the ambulance arrived. How they got through the parting I'll never know, but the tragedy of it will be with me all my life."

What a story that is. In the main, I think, I have tried to remind folk that there is still something wonderful in life . . . but I pass on this story because it is perhaps a good thing for us to realise now and then what suffering there is, and how unspeakably bleak life can sometimes be for others.

Some Ten-Second Sermons:

It is easy to make allowances for our faults, but dangerous; hard to make allowances for other's faults, but wise.

When you see a good man, think of emulating him; when you see a bad man, examine your own heart.

Life is like playing a violin solo in public and learning the instrument as one plays it.

The business of life is to go forward.

SATURDAY—FEBRUARY 19.

I LIKE schoolboy howlers. Here are a few.

The principal thing which was left behind by the Egyptians was their bones.

On one side of a penny is the Queen's head, on the other a young lady riding a bicycle ; they call her Ruby Tanyer.

The navy is sometimes called the Senile Service.

Tarzan is a short name for the American flag. It's full name is Tarzan Stripes.

Glaziers are common, they move about one foot per day in Switzerland.

SUNDAY—FEBRUARY 20.

THE things which are impossible with men are possible with God.

MONDAY—FEBRUARY 21.

ONE of my treasures is a small white card with a few raised dots. The dots are arranged to make curious, though simple shapes, thus :

The card came to me from Canada, a gift I shall always keep because it has a special interest to me —it's my name, Francis Gay, in Braille.

Time and time again every day I write my name with a pen—it takes next to no time to do it, and I can see it when it is done.

But round the world are millions of blind folk, old and young, rich and poor. What a loss is theirs —missing the everyday things you and I see and enjoy. Everyday things—but how empty life could be without them.

THE FRIENDSHIP BOOK

MAY was a girl of 19 when she became seriously ill with pneumonia.

By what seemed a miracle, she pulled through —but in the five months that followed, she took pleurisy, scarlet fever, diphtheria, and rheumatic fever, and her weight fell to four stones! When at last she was allowed home from hospital, she was told her heart had been badly damaged by all the illness she'd suffered, and that to marry and have children might kill her.

But she decided it was a risk she would take —and she and her husband were blessed with two children. At length, however, her health grew so bad she had to spend most of the day in bed. Then, in 1954, she was told she could have an operation. There was only a 50-50 chance of success, but if she refused it she would be a semi-invalid all her life.

Well, she went through with the operation—and, glory be, it was a complete success. Now she leads a normal life again.

But best of all, she spends four nights a week nursing in a hospital, seeking to use the life that was given to her, in the service of other folk—and I know she brings to her work there a sympathy and understanding born of all she has been through herself.

THE winter sky was coldly grey
    When these small ladies came to stay,
    So much to my delight.
So sweet and good and modest, they
All whispered, " Spring is on the way "—
    My snowdrops, green and white!

THE FRIENDSHIP BOOK

Thursday—February 24.

THE great artist Joseph Mallord William Turner did a very big thing once without brush or paint.

He was then a member of the hanging committee of the Royal Academy. One day, when the annual exhibition was about to open, and all the walls were filled with pictures, Turner happened to come across a picture which had been submitted but overlooked. It was by an unknown artist in the provinces.

" This picture must be shown," declared Turner.

" Impossible," said the rest of the committee. " All the wall space is now covered, and there is no time . . . "

But Turner did not wait to hear what they had to say. In his forthright way, he strode across the salon, calmly took down one of his own exhibits, and hung the picture by an unknown artist in its place.

Surely that was true greatness—and a challenge to you and to me to do what we think needs to be done, even if it is going to cost us something.

Friday—February 25.

I KNOW very well that the worst of the winter may be ahead, that we may have snow or winds or ice or storms that will be talked of a hundred years ahead — I know, I know it very well.

But does morning come just a minute or two sooner now? Is it light a minute or two longer in the afternoon? Did I hear some excited chatter among the sparrows the other day? Could the shops be showing spring-time fashions?

Most probably it is my vivid imagination—but at any rate, we're heading for spring-time rather than autumn, aren't we?

AS WE SHOULD BE . . .

He never passes on a bend
    Nor ordained speeds exceedeth:
Treats other drivers as his friend
    And right of way concedeth.
I met a chap like that—but there!
    I scarcely can remember where.

DAVID HOPE

THE CARVER

He hewed them from a loftier plain,
These crags which now we climb,
And smoothed them with the wind and rain
In a million years of time.

How right that we with humble heart
Should peak and gully scan.
Yet sigh not for our fleeting part:
No! Praise the Master Plan.

DAVID HOPE

THE END OF THE DAY

We've seen some service, Bess and me,
An' I reckon we've done our best.
It's a long road we've travelled, an' I don't see
You mindin' us takin' a rest.

DAVID HOPE

THE FRIENDSHIP BOOK

SOME folk seem to think of eventide homes as cheerless places—but I've been in a few, and I know better.

I'm thinking, for example, of a story from an eventide home where, some years ago, a group of old folk were sitting by the fire talking to the superintendent and matron.

As it sometimes does, the conversation turned to funerals. One old lady turned to the superintendent and asked him if he'd do something for her when she died. " It's my letters from Bob," she confided. " They're all upstairs, tied with ribbon—and when I go I'd like you to put them in beside me before I'm buried . . . "

It was a touching thought that the old soul had kept her man's letters for more than 50 years—but the mood was quickly dispelled by Granny Brown.

" Yes," she said with a grin, " and you'd better put in a candle and some matches, or else she won't be able to read them !"

LORD, what wilt Thou have me to do?

IN his long life, Sir Winston wrote or said a great many things worth remembering, and one of the wittiest and wisest of all his remarks was, surely—
We are all worms, but I think I am a glow worm.

You and I may agree that we live in a dark world, and we may even humble ourselves enough to acknowledge that we are nobody very much . . . but even if we are worms, let's be glow worms, and light the darkness just a bit.

MARCH

I KNOW a young couple who, you would have said, had everything.

They were happily married with two fine boys. The husband had a good job, and soon they were to move into a house of their own. Indeed, they counted themselves richly blessed.

Then their younger son, aged four, was taken to hospital seriously ill. Within six days he was dead.

But worse was to follow, for a few months later they lost their second child.

To add to their sorrow, the doctor told the mother she must never have another baby.

Yet, I know that their new home echoes again to shouts of glee and the laughter of children. For they decided, even in their grief, that there were many homeless children who needed the love they'd had for their own boys, and they have taken two handicapped brothers into their home to fill the gap that was left.

A brave step—yet I know they are finding something of the joy that was once theirs, and the pride that only parenthood can bring.

I F you've never helped another
  When the road was pretty steep,
If you've never shared a burden,
  Never lost a bit of sleep
Over someone else's trouble,
  Never smiled though heart was sore,
May I ask you, quite politely,
  " What are you around here for ?"

ROBERT REID, of Dundee, was all his days a stalwart of the Boys' Brigade. He was 86 when his brave march ended, and by his wise and faithful example, he helped hundreds of lads to trust in God and do the right. To all of them he was simply "The Skipper."

At his funeral, the church was crowded with men and boys he had set on the right road. The youngest was 14, the oldest a man in his 80's.

It was a moving sight as six stalwart men, who had once been his boys, bore him through the ranks for the last time, and there were tears in many an eye as the minister spoke of the splendid life they had gathered to honour.

Then, as one, men and boys rose to join in one of his favourite hymns, a great promise upon which he had founded his faith. No farewell could have been more fitting to a life that helped to mould the characters of so many boys—

There is a land of pure delight,
Where saints immortal reign;
Infinite day excludes the night,
And pleasures banish pain . . .

WHILE chatting the other day with a minister I know well, he happened to say that his was a 24-hour-a-day job, and he summed it up very neatly, or so I thought, in these words:—

"In the pulpit I preach the gospel—that is, the good news of the saving power of Jesus Christ our Lord; and out of it I minister as best I can to the young, to the old, to the troubled, the lonely, and the sad."

What a great and glorious task is his!

THE FRIENDSHIP BOOK

SATURDAY—MARCH 5.

THE other day I came across a big truth in a short sentence. It is a challenging thought—and there is more to it than meets the eye. Young folk can afford to ignore it, but those of us who are not so young as we used to be would do well to keep it in mind, and, indeed, to think about it quite often.

The sentence, written by a Frenchman, Andre Maurois, is this:—Growing old is no more than a bad habit which a busy man has no time to form.

SUNDAY—MARCH 6.

THE Lord shall preserve thee from all evil: He shall preserve thy soul.

MONDAY—MARCH 7.

THE Lady of the House has a new job.

Recently Granny Brodie came to live with her eldest son and his wife, less than half a mile from our door. She is happy as the day is long, is well cared for and much loved, and has a charming room all to herself in a very gracious house.

But as yet very few people know her. She is unable to go out, so she has few visitors.

And there is one thing she likes doing more than anything else in the world—reading aloud the weekly letters from her other four sons or their wives. But people don't read letters aloud unless there is somebody to read them to—so once a week the Lady of the House calls to see Granny Brodie, shares a cup of tea, has a chat about things, and then sits back in her chair and listens !

Well, it's a pleasant, comfy job by a friendly fire —and what a thrill for Granny Brodie to have somebody listening to four letters a week !

TUESDAY—MARCH 8.

ONE afternoon—wet and windy and very cold—
the Lady of the House popped in to have a few
words with one of her old dears. She found Mrs
Craig standing at the rain-washed window.

" Oh, hello," said my wife. " You can't go out
on a day like this !"

" That's lucky !" replied Mrs Craig, aged 86.
" I was just looking out to see if I might venture as
far as the shops at the corner, and when I saw the
rain coming down and heard the wind, I was so
thankful I couldn't go ! I always find that when the
weather's too bad for me to go out, that's the time
I just don't want to go !"

What a genius for being content old Mrs Craig
has !

WEDNESDAY—MARCH 9.

SIR, why not buy a bunch or two
Of springtime flowers fair ?
And take them home one winter's day
(But carry them with care);
Just hand them to your wife and say—
I thought of you in town today !

THURSDAY—MARCH 10.

FROM a housewife comes a verse of only two
lines which, she assures me, has helped her on
her way many a time when the going was not easy.

She tells me she is apt to get as weary of the chores
as anybody else, but she assures me that she has the
modern woman's philosophy, and that it is all
summed up in this couplet—

Since woman's work is never done,
Let's do our best to make it fun !

THE FRIENDSHIP BOOK

IT has become a kind of ritual now . . .

Every so often it is my happy privilege to entertain two laddies on a Sunday afternoon. And every time I do so they repay me by tormenting me with riddles which I simply can't puzzle out.

" Mr Gay," said one, " can you turn 999 into 100 by adding another 9 ?" Reaching for pencil and paper, I proceeded to try to work it out. But, oh, dear, in the end I had to confess it had me beaten.

" It's simple," my tormentor grinned—and with a flourish he scribbled down the answer, 99 9-9ths.

You should have seen the despairing look I gave the boys—but, between you and me, it wouldn't be half the fun for them OR me if I knew the answers to their conundrums. For the sight of their triumphant faces when they know they've done it again is worth a thousand inglorious defeats !

YEARS ago William Beebe, the famous American writer, and his friend, President Theodore Roosevelt, used often to play a little game which was all their own. Both were much in the public eye. Each had many a chance to show off; but always after an hour or two's chat in the evening they would go out of doors, look up at the night sky, search for a star in the left-hand corner of Pegasus, and recite together:—

" That is the spiral galaxy of Andromeda.

It is as large as our Milky Way.

It is one of a hundred million galaxies——"

Then Beebe and Roosevelt would grin at each other, and the President would remark—" Well, I guess we both feel small enough now. Let's go to bed !"

THE FRIENDSHIP BOOK

SUNDAY—MARCH 13.

THE Lord thy God in the midst of thee is mighty ;
He will save, He will rejoice over thee with joy.

MONDAY—MARCH 14.

IN 1945, Bill lost one of his legs. Two years later
his other leg had to be removed. For months
on end he lay between life and death, and to this day
there are two and a half years of which he can
remember nothing.

Only his determination to live carried him
through. Ever since, Bill has spent most of his life
in his wheelchair, and that is why cutting the grass
is such a triumph for him.

It's a painful job and he can cover only a few
yards at a time. Others have offered to do it for him,
but Bill, determined fellow that he is, prefers to
do it himself, even though it takes him more than
a week.

You'll never see a statue of Bill, yet who can deny
that, in his own way, he is one of the quiet heroes
who go on, year after year, fighting their own private
battles—and winning them magnificently.

TUESDAY—MARCH 15.

IT makes all the difference how you look at things
today. Keep a sharp eye wide open for the ugly
things, the unpleasant things, the tiresome things—
and you will go to bed tonight disgusted with living.

But if from morning till evening today you are
looking for the good, ready to enjoy whatever little
bit of fortune comes your way, why, you will go
to bed thanking God that, after all, this is really not
a bad world to live in.

Try it.

THE FRIENDSHIP BOOK

*THAT sunny day she plodded on, no joy in her
    old heart,
She felt unwanted in the crowd with which she
    had no part;
Then suddenly, " Hello, Hello ! It's lovely seeing
    YOU !"
And one old heart was young again—that
    SOMEONE cared, she knew !*

OLD Sandy Gregory had been an organist for
more than 60 years.

At Rothesay and then at Comrie, until he was 76,
he charmed folk with the magic of his fingers.

Then old Sandy fell ill and in his heart he realised
the end could not be far off.

Yet, during his years at the organ he had found
something to give him strength just when it was
most needed. It was Hymn 174, his favourite
above all others—" Rest of the weary, Joy of the
sad."

Every day during his illness Sandy turned up
his hymn and read the simple, comforting words—

" Home of the stranger, Strength to the end,
Refuge from danger, Saviour and Friend . . ."

There, indeed, Sandy found a peace which was
with him to the end. For when he died, his hymn
book was found by his side, and it lay open at his
favourite hymn.

That is why it was sung at his funeral and why
his many friends sang it again on the Sunday
morning in the kirk he had served so well. To those
who took part in the services, the hymn, with its
deep, quiet assurance, seemed almost a benediction
from the old man who had gone.

HOUSE OF CARDS

" Patience is a virtue," my father used to say,
" But it needs a lot of practice," he'd explain ;
" When everything collapses — as it might for you one day —
You have to learn to build it up again."

DAVID HOPE

C

THE PEACE OF THE HILLS

There's a silence in the mountains,
A peace which eases pain,
A solitude, enabling us to see
The loveliness and sorrow,
The problems of tomorrow,
Reminding us that what will be — will be.

DAVID HOPE

THE FRIENDSHIP BOOK

WHENEVER you hear or see or read the news and feel disturbed because there are so many bad people and there is so much suffering and foolishness, don't get too depressed. Remember this :—The worst is always much more in evidence than the best. It is the thieves who get into the news — honest folk are never (or very rarely) mentioned. A man may have half a column of news for being drunk or disorderly, but he can be sober and decent and law-abiding and useful for half a century and never earn even one line in the local Press. The mad goings-on of silly young people make headlines, but how often do the quiet, decent, friendly young men and women get into the news ?

Keep this in mind — it will help you to see the picture as a whole.

JAMES CAIRNS passed on recently, leaving a cherished memory, for though he had more troubles than most of us he never lost his ability to smile along, never forgot to be hopeful and always saw the bright side of things.

If I were to say that Jim was all his life a preacher he would be vastly amused, for as far as I know he never once went up into a pulpit. Yet he did preach by being Jim Cairns, the man whom we remember— among other things—for his quaint trick in wet or windy or unpleasant weather. If ever you met Jim in the rain, and said, " Isn't it awful ?" he would grin happily and reply—" We'll be having better weather pretty soon !"

That was Jim's theme, his religion, his philosophy, his challenge . . . things may be bad just now, but they'll get better if you keep on. They always do !

SUNDAY—MARCH 20.

ASK, and it shall be given you ; seek, and ye shall find.

MONDAY—MARCH 21.

"OH, dear," said an Aberdeen woman the other day, "if I were to think of all the unkind things that have been done to me and said about me, and the way people have taken me in and caused no end of trouble or have promised to do a job for me and have either never done it or done it badly, why, I should just sit down and cry and cry for ever.

"But, of course," she added, " I never do sit down and think about all such things. Where's the sense ? Who wants to weep for ever . . . and how impatient my family and friends would be if I did that kind of thing !"

TUESDAY—MARCH 22.

IN the glow of an oil lamp, a young mother is teaching her little ones to say their prayers. It is a picture of perfect happiness and peace.

But the joy of that family was soon to be darkened, for, two days before her youngest child's first birthday, the mother died. She was only 25. Yet the magic of that quiet moment in the manse lives on. For the mother who passed away so suddenly was Mary Lundie Duncan, who wrote this hymn for her children.

Jesus, tender Shepherd, hear me;
Bless Thy little lamb tonight;
Through the darkness be Thou near me,
Watch my sleep till morning light.

She never knew, of course, that her simple lines would one day be treasured by so many—yet how happy the knowledge would have made her.

THE FRIENDSHIP BOOK

NOW what do the little birds say as they chirp
so high on a branch in the sun?
They chatter and chatter and bob their small heads
—has something exciting begun?
Maybe they are telling each other the news: Sing
loudly in sunshine and rain.
Sing merrily on for the storm clouds are gone—
and now it is springtime again!

CAN you imagine placing a bet of £500 on a horse?

I confess, I can't.

Yet here's a man who actually did this day after day, winning and losing thousands of pounds without batting an eyelid.

His name is Victor McManus, and he's as Irish as the Mountains of Mourne, where he was born. His family were well to do, with a chain of shops that, if he wished, would one day be his. But Victor had other ideas. While still in his early twenties, he entered the world of horse racing and all that it means.

Then one night in his hotel bedroom, his wallet bulging with £400 he had won that afternoon, he saw himself as he really was.

It was the turning point of his life. He gave up everything he had once prized, made up his mind to devote his life to others, and entered college to train as a missionary.

That was almost twenty years ago. Today Victor McManus influences the lives of thousands all over the world. He visits schools, hospitals, factories, even prisons, proclaiming the faith that changed his life.

FRIDAY—MARCH 25.

MORE than a hundred years ago, a boy started work in a pawnbroker's shop.

Young as he was, his heart was touched by the desperate plight of the poor folk, who tried to pawn almost anything they had to buy food for themselves and their families. A year later, the boy's father died, and his own mother and sisters found themselves left in poverty.

While still in his teens the boy began preaching in the streets of Nottingham, and at 20 he was proclaiming his message of hope and faith in London, where he was pelted with cabbages and rotten eggs for his pains. But, undaunted, he set up a mission of his own.

His name was William Booth, and from these humble beginnings sprang the great mission of mercy we know today as the Salvation Army. For 100 years it has fought to let light into dark places in many lands.

SATURDAY—MARCH 26.

SHE has five lovely children—the youngest still only seven.

That means they are a big family in a small house, and their father is by no means a rich man, but I do not know where you will find seven happier folk or a family that likes being together so much and gets along so well. Squalls are scarce, smiles plentiful—a truly lovable company of willing, friendly folk.

And if you ask Mum how she manages to look after her squad, and why they all pull together, and what is the secret of her success in the home, she will smile and say, " Oh, well, I expect it's just because I love them—and they know it."

THE FRIENDSHIP BOOK

DELIVER my soul, O Lord, from lying lips, and from a deceitful tongue.

MANY stories are told of Dr Spurgeon, the great London preacher; this is my favourite.

He was speaking to a group of young ministers, passing on to them some of the secrets of a successful sermon, and he gave them this advice.

" My friends, when you talk to your congregation about heaven, let your faces light up with joy and shine with a heavenly gladness.

" When you talk to them about hell, your ordinary faces will do . . . !"

THIS little poem, a prayer of the very old, was passed on to me by a friend.

Blessed are they who understand
My faltering step and shaking hand;
Blessed, who know my ears today
Must strain to catch the things they say.
Blessed are they who seem to know
My eyes are dim and my mind is slow;
Blessed are they who looked away
When tea spilled on the cloth that day.
Blessed are they with a cheery smile,
Who stopped to chat for a little while;
Blessed are those who never say,
" You've told that story twice today."
Blessed are they who make it known
That I'm loved, respected, and not alone;
And blessed are they who ease the days
Of my journey home, in loving ways.

THE FRIENDSHIP BOOK

HOW Granny LOVES the springtime!
 The days are longer now;
And, sitting at her window,
 She'll wave to folk or bow.
And they smile back at Granny;
 The children running by . . .
Old folk are not so lonely
 When sunny is the sky!

SUMMER and winter Wullie McCulloch tramps the lonely Border byways around Penicuik, his pack on his back and his staff in his hand—but every few weeks he turns up on the doorstep of the manse in the village of Carlops.

There's always a welcome there for him and he is always an honoured guest at the table of the minister, Rev. Alexander Caseby. Why? Because Mr Caseby is one of those rare men to whom no one is a stranger.

But there is another reason. Fifty years ago, when both Wullie and Mr Caseby were young men, they spent three and a half years on the battlefields of France and Flanders. Both knew the horrors and the comradeship of the trenches, both saw their friends fall by their side—it was this common experience that started their friendship.

So now, in the evening, they often sit by the fireside, not as minister and tramp, but as two old soldiers sharing the same memories. That is why, somewhere in his pack, Wullie has placed a little note asking that, should anything happen to him, he wants Mr Caseby to take his funeral service.

When the time comes, Mr Caseby will be proud to honour the last will of his old comrade.

APRIL

I OPENED a book on Persia and found thirteen words which seemed to be the key to a lost world.

I say a lost world, for I am thinking of the world of art—a lovely, colourful, enriching, pleasing, satisfying world glowing with brightness, the kind of art which very few modern artists have patience to attempt. I do not condemn because a thing happens to be modern, but I do feel that the rank and file of us are poorer because so much so-called art is quickly and carelessly done daubing, whereas years ago skill and patience and something like devotion and inspiration went towards the creation of a thing of beauty.

And so, it seems, it was in ancient Persia, for somewhere in that wonderful country we can find, carved in stone, these words—*Whatever works seem beautiful, we did it all by the grace of God.*

I RAISE my hat to three Wishaw girls. They are Mary, Margaret, and Isabel, all in their 20's.

All three waved good-bye to their friends, their families, their homes, and all the familiar things that mean most in life—for they decided to become missionaries in Africa and to devote the rest of their lives to carrying the banner of their faith there.

Mary was a teacher, Margaret was a clerkess, and Isabel was a nurse. They were happy in their careers, yet each felt something vital was missing. After deep thought and earnest prayer, they knew this was the only answer to what they sought.

It's to folk like these three girls that we owe much of the grand heritage of this country of ours.

THE FRIENDSHIP BOOK

HE that believeth on Me hath everlasting life.

"WHAT sort of a doctor is he?"
    "Well, I don't know much about his ability, but he's got a very good bedside manner."

This appeared as a cartoon in "Punch" and ever since it has been chuckled over by people who have said shrewdly, "What's the use of a doctor who has only a good bedside manner?"

But I would like to turn this round, suggesting that while what we need first and foremost in a medical man is knowledge and skill, these are not enough by themselves.

And I'm not thinking of doctors only. I'm thinking of people who speak the truth, but not quite as graciously as they might; of people who do good, but don't do it as diplomatically as they ought; of folk who are strictly correct, but lack just that human touch and that bit of humour which help so much to warm the heart and make life worthwhile. There's a lot to be said for that bedside manner.

"SOME of us," said the preacher, "have queer notions about life and ourselves. Most of us really do believe that circumstances are harder for us than they are for other people, and we are so busy bemoaning the fact that we miss quite a lot of the good which might otherwise come our way . . .

"Each of us thinks his lot the worst—but he's mistaken. If he thought himself the worst of the lot, he might be right . . . and God might have a chance to make something worthwhile of him!"

THE FRIENDSHIP BOOK

So you're finding life hard? I don't wonder.
There are these kind of days for us all.
But I bet you will never go under
If you keep someone else from a fall.

THE night nurse dimmed the lights and sat down at her table to keep her vigil through the long, dark hours. All round, there was silence.

Suddenly, a voice began to speak through the ward. It was old Mrs Stephen, saying her prayers. She was gravely ill, yet every night without fail, she prayed aloud while the ward listened.

The nurse would lay down her pen, or her book, to join with bowed head in the old lady's simple prayer.

Reverently, Mrs Stephen asked God to bless her beloved man, her home, her own folk, and her neighbours. Then she prayed for her church, for her minister, and for the minister's wife. She never forgot the hospital, either—the ward where she lay, those who lay around her, and all the doctors and nurses who looked after them.

Last of all there was a wee prayer for herself, that she might be brave enough to face whatever might be asked of her. And when the " Amen " came, unseen lips echoed it, and a peace that was not of this world settled over the ward like a benediction.

Did Mrs Stephen ever realise how many were with her when she met with her Maker each night before she slept ? I will never know, for she passed away quietly.

But I do know that those who prayed with her saw the real meaning of faith and infinite trust, and it was an experience they will never forget.

THE FRIENDSHIP BOOK

ALMIGHTY God, Father of all mercies, we, Thine unworthy servants, do give Thee humble and hearty thanks for all Thy goodness and loving kindness to us, and to all men. We thank Thee for our creation, preservation, and all the blessings of this life; but above all for Thine inestimable love in the redemption of the world by our Lord Jesus Christ; for the means of grace and for the hope of glory.

And, we beseech Thee, give us that due sense of all Thy mercies that our hearts may be unfeignedly thankful, and that we may show forth Thy praise not only with our lips but in our lives, by giving up ourselves to Thy service, and by walking before Thee in holiness and righteousness all our days.

MAKING a success of living is never easy no matter how rich or poor you are.

Some people are very religious, yet seem to miss the joys they were meant to know. Some folk are easy-going, and fail to do anything much either for themselves or for the happiness of others. Some people always seem to do the wrong thing.

There is no royal road to a happy and useful life, unless it is the one which is so simple and obvious that far too many of us travel a long way without ever realising it.

It was summed up for me long ago by a wise, but happy man who never went to university. " Laddie," he said, " as you go along the road, hold fast to God with one hand, and open wide the other to your neighbour."

Don't make the mistake of thinking this too elementary.

SUNDAY—APRIL 10.

THEN said Jesus, Father forgive them ; for they know not what they do.

MONDAY—APRIL 11.

IN my reading I came across a short sentence by Christopher Morley, which made me consider a long time.

" Only the sinner has the right to preach."

Surely Morley is wrong ? Surely it is the saints, the very good people, who should preach ?

Or is Morley right ? How can any man preach in a pulpit if he has never done wrong, never been sorry for his sins, never had to fight to keep himself from wrong-doing or speaking or thinking ? Is it not out of his struggles towards perfection, however short a distance he has got, that he learns the true meaning and cost of fine living, and is aware of the boundless love and saving grace of God ?

TUESDAY—APRIL 12.

I TRUST my golfing friends will pardon me for quoting here a little rhyme I came across the other day—no offence intended, of course, and if I've played into the hands of the non-golfing wives, I apologise.

> Last night I had a funny pain,
>   And to the doc I flew.
> Said he, " This comes from overwork—
>   There's nothing I can do.
> You need a month of quiet rest,"
>   He added with a smile.
> " You'd better drop your golf and try
>   The office for a while."

WEDNESDAY—APRIL 13.

TODAY we had an April shower,
  It only lasted half an hour,
The sky was grey and sad.

But now the sky is bright and gay,
It's going to be a lovely day!
The birds and I are glad.

THURSDAY—APRIL 14.

FOR years the Rev. Angus Macaskill had ministered faithfully. By his kindliness and shining faith he had built up his congregation until it numbered 2000.

No man could have loved his church more than Mr Macaskill, and it was that which led him to make way for a young man to carry on the work.

I know it was no easy decision, nor was it easy for Mr Macaskill when his flock gathered to bid him farewell. The church was crowded, and for the last time Mr Macaskill raised his hands in blessing, and pronounced the benediction. Then, as he turned to descend from the pulpit, the choir began to sing, soft as a whisper—

God be with you till we meet again,
  By His counsels guide, uphold you,
  With His sheep securely fold you,
God be with you till we meet again.

It was the perfect farewell. Before Mr Macaskill reached the last step of the pulpit, the tears were running unchecked down his face, and he was not ashamed of them. For he knew it was not simply a last tribute from the choir, but a prayer for him that was echoed in every soul there.

Surely they could not have found a lovelier way of expressing it.

FRIDAY—APRIL 15.

A FRIEND decided to have a day's fishing, and was out of bed very early on a fine spring morning. Before sunrise he was marching down to the river, carrying his tackle and his breakfast and lunch, and perhaps just the least bit proud of himself for having rolled out of bed at such an unearthly hour.

How pleasant to hum a merry tune as he walked in an utterly lonely world!

At a bend in the road he came face to face with a dairyman. "Good morning, good morning," breezed the happy angler. "It's nice to be up and about early on a fine morning!"

"Yes," muttered the dairyman. "Yes, it looks like being a bit of fair weather—but it was cold first thing!"

SATURDAY—APRIL 16.

I THINK it's one of the loveliest stories I've come across for a long time.

It seems a woman got off a bus at a fare stage and asked somebody—"Do you know when there will be a bus to Clifton?"

"It should be here in five minutes," said the bystander. Then he thought for a moment. "Excuse me," he said at last, "the bus you've just left was going to Clifton. Why did you get off?"

The lady coloured slightly. "Oh," she began, "I just sort of thought I would." As this sounded too silly for words, she went on—"The fact is, at the last fare stage a man with crutches got on and the bus was full. I didn't want to embarrass him by offering him my seat, so I just stood up and pretended I'd reached my destination. That's all."

SUNDAY—APRIL 17.

A MAN that hath friends must shew himself friendly : and there is a friend that sticketh closer than a brother.

MONDAY—APRIL 18.

MY doorbell rang.

Dutifully, I rose to answer it, wondering who on earth could have braved such a wet night to call on me. And when I opened the door, there was a ten-year-old boy, with the rain streaming down his face, his coat soaked and his feet in a puddle.

But did he mind? Not a bit, for his eyes were shining with excitement. "Come in!" I cried, and while I helped him off with his dripping coat, I discovered the reason for his visit.

He simply wanted to show me his school report card! Pulling it from his pocket, he gave it to me and waited, his face aglow, while I settled down to read it.

What pleased me every bit as much as the marks themselves—or maybe even more—was the fact that a good report meant so much to him, and that he'd been so proud of it that, after showing it to his parents, he'd run smiling through the rain to let me have a look at it, too.

TUESDAY—APRIL 19.

THOSE of us who have a multitude of things to do may well pray this simple prayer:—

Give to me, Lord, a quiet mind
When pressing duties throng;
A peaceful mien, a gentle voice,
And strength to carry on.

THE FRIENDSHIP BOOK

SOME folk are very hard to please,
 That fact there's no denying;
And there are folk can't see a joke,
 And folk that are most trying.
Such folk I meet—oh, every day . . .
 Yet sweet is self-deception;
From truth I shrink, and like to think
 I am the one exception!

HIS name was Sandy Mackenzie, but I cannot tell you where he lived, for he was a tinker and his home was wherever he pitched his tent.

I met him by chance some years ago on the road, and though I could never have lived his kind of life, there was something about him that made me remember him.

He couldn't read or write, and he wouldn't have known his own name if he had seen it before him. So, when he was called upon to write his signature, he made a mark like (as he put it) the cross of Jesus lying on its side.

But he knew every flower that bloomed by the wayside, he could tell each bird by its song, and one glance at the sun told him the exact time of day. These were the things that mattered to him.

That was Sandy's life, and for nearly 80 years he lived it happily. Then he fell ill. He was brought to the cottage hospital, and before dawn broke next morning he had passed on. Strangely, the only night he spent in a real bed turned out to be his last.

He was laid to rest in the little cemetery at Aberfeldy, and, as if by magic, tinkers from far and near came to pay him tribute. He was truly one of nature's gentlemen.

FRIDAY—APRIL 22.

ONE of the best things about daffodils is—they're useless!

That's odd, I hear you say. But, when you think of it, what can you do with a bunch or two of daffodils except look at them? Nobody cooks or eats them. You can't use the dried stems to make baskets. Oh, I dare say there are some uses, but, in a general way, daffodils are lovely flowers —and that's it.

Now, don't you think this is significant? It means, for instance, life is more than materialism, more than utility, more than we can weigh or measure . . . for surely it's true to say no man or woman ever really lives if they have no love of lovely things, no awareness of things spiritual, no sense of wonder—or find no joy in just looking at daffodils.

SATURDAY—APRIL 23.

MAY I introduce you to " Sir " Jim and his white charger?

Actually, "Sir" Jim's name is Jim Hogg, and he lives in Scotland. Everybody who knows him admires him.

You see, due to an illness, Jim had to lose both his legs, and though that must be a hard blow for any man to bear, it was doubly so for Jim, for he was never one to be idle.

But despite his handicap, Jim made a tour of England, visiting his daughters and relations. He went as far south as Kent, then came back up the west coast—and he did the whole journey alone in his invalid car, a round trip of well over 1000 miles!

I reckon even St George's slaying of the dragon was no prouder feat than this journey of Jim's. That's why I salute him for a splendid victory.

A MATTER OF TASTE

They say that we're the farmers' friend,
The grubs we eat they know no end.
Oh lucky man, that rooks are born,
Preferring wireworms to corn.

DAVID HOPE

WINTER

Where sighing trees bend to the wind's cold breath,
  Where forlorn hills sweep downward to the glen;
Where winter seems to bring a touch of death—
  I know the summer sun will shine again.

DAVID HOPE

SUNDAY—APRIL 24.

A MERRY heart doeth good like a medicine.

MONDAY—APRIL 25.

MARY lives in an old house in a very drab street. Walk along that street and you realise that it has an air of decay. It is growing older and shabbier . . . except one house, and that one house has a clean step, bright yellow door, and windows which shine and have clean curtains.

Inside every room is papered and painted by Mary. Every floor carpeted. Every inch spotless.

And all because Mary, wife of a man who, not being very strong, has only a light and, therefore, a rather poorly-paid job, manages so amazingly. Not only can she wash and cook and make her own clothes—she is handy with tools, and can paper and paint. She can buy an old chest of drawers and make a lovely bit of furniture of it. She can do wonders—and can do them with a smile.

Secret ? Years ago she realised that there was no escaping housework. " So I just made up my mind to like it," she told me.

TUESDAY—APRIL 26.

WHEN you get a touch of sunshine in the morning, and if there happens to be a fair bit of blue sky and there's a patch of dry road and a fresh wind, and if you happen—on the way to work—to hear a few birds singing and you have spotted one or two green shoots in the garden—well, it isn't very hard to whistle as you stride along, is it ?

But, of course, the really big thing to do is to whistle as you go along even when there isn't a sign of springtime anywhere !

WEDNESDAY—APRIL 27.

WEE JIM is all for sport, of course—
An ardent football fan;
But often, home from school, he'll make
Some welcome toast for Gran.
And Granny says, " No toast could be
As nice as what Jim makes for me !"

THURSDAY—APRIL 28.

LAST century a Scottish minister died young, leaving his widow with three boys. She was as poor as poor, but she resolved that, God willing, her boys should enter the Church. That meant, of course, that not one of them would earn a penny before he was turned 25 or 26 at the earliest. On the face of it, it couldn't be done. But it was done.

She brought up her sons to enjoy a frugal life, to study hard, to love all things good and true. In 1905 she moved to Edinburgh so that all three of her boys could go to the University. How grim life must have been for that family of four—or so you might think when you learn that even in their teens Donald, Peter, and John never had a penny to spare. But you would be wrong. They enjoyed life, made wonderful friendships, and thought nothing of going to bed late and rising early.

But the miracle of their mother's dream came true. One of her lads became a missionary doctor, and the other two ministers identified themselves with St Andrews University and Edinburgh University, each a professor, honoured and loved.

I feel that the splendid and useful lives of Donald, Peter, and John Baillie were the result of a mother's prayers. Surely there is need today for something of that glorious faith she had, that selfless devotion which was part of her very life ?

THE FRIENDSHIP BOOK

ONE Sunday morning the Rev. John A. Paterson spoke to the children about the little chap who asked his Sunday school teacher if the Eastern shepherds had dogs.

His teacher said she would try to find out for the following Sunday.

She was forestalled by the little fellow, who met his teacher later and said, ' I know they had dogs, for the shepherd who wrote the 23rd Psalm had two and I even know their names, Goodness and Mercy, for in the last verse it says " Goodness and Mercy shall follow me all the days of my life and I will dwell in the House of the Lord for ever." '

A lady came to the minister after the service and thanked him for the story, which was new to her, but she added, ' Do you know, I found a third dog in that verse; and its name is " Surely."

' Surely Goodness and Mercy shall follow me all the days of my life !' When you come to think of it ' Surely ' is worth remembering, for God, the Great Shepherd, is sure in all His ways.

DON'T be surprised if one of these days you find I have been arrested for assault and battery !

I'll have made mincemeat of that young scamp, Robert, who only the other morning was up to his tricks again, asking me if I knew where to find elephants.

I launched into a lecture on Africa, only to be pulled up short by—" You're wrong, Mr Gay. You don't find them anywhere—they're too big to get lost !" And off he went, whistling.

Oh, how I wish we could all be as young and lively.

MAY

SUNDAY—MAY 1.

LET the heavens be glad, and let the earth rejoice: and let men say among the nations, the Lord reigneth.

MONDAY—MAY 2.

THIS is the story of the one-ton problem.

It all began when a minister found some old houses were being demolished and asked if he might have the floorboards, planks, and beams as firewood for his old folk. A few hours later a lorry pulled up at the church and tipped a ton of timber into the road.

It was only then the problem struck the minister. Here he was on his own, faced with a pile of wood as high as a house that had to be shifted into the yard behind the church.

But he took off his collar, rolled up his sleeves, and got to work. Alas, the more wood he moved the more there seemed to be, and he began to wonder if he'd ever finish!

Then two boys stepped forward. They'd been watching—and they asked if they could help. A few minutes later another boy appeared—and another —until there were no fewer than ten boys lending a hand.

After that the rest was easy. The pile of wood vanished like magic from the street and reappeared neatly stacked in the yard. And ten wee boys found themselves clutching a bar of chocolate—a present from a grateful minister who, but for them, might still have been busy at midnight.

One-ton problem, did I say? I beg your pardon. I should have said the one-ton triumph!

TUESDAY—MAY 3.

ANDREW BAIN never wastes a minute, but always has time for a wee chat with anybody.

He had been going around Falkirk taking colour photographs of what is old and new; and during one of these excursions he walked hurriedly through the kirkyard to take a snap before the sun went behind a cloud.

As it happened, the postie was also taking a short cut through the kirkyard; and Andrew Bain just couldn't resist the temptation to say—" I didn't know you had any customers here !"

That's Andrew all over. No wonder folk go on their way chuckling after meeting him !

WEDNESDAY—MAY 4.

IF you have lost all you held dear,
If threatening is your sky,
Do not despair and do not sit
For ever asking, " Why ?"
Just by keeping on you may
See midnight wear to dawn one day.

THURSDAY—MAY 5.

I FANCY the most logical thinkers are small children. I felt even more sure of this the other day when I heard about a boy of three and a bit.

When a neighbour met him one morning she chatted about this and that, and then, to keep the conversation going, she asked the little chap how old he was. " Two," he replied promptly.

The lady smiled as she murmured, " Oh, no. I think you are older than that."

Without batting an eyelid, the small boy replied, " Yes, I is. But I can't say fwee !"

FRIDAY—MAY 6.

A READER sends me this verse which I am happy to pass on:

Pray don't find fault with the man who limps
Or stumbles along the road,
Unless you have worn the shoes he wears,
Or struggled beneath his load,
There may be nails in his shoes that hurt,
Though hidden away from view;
Or the burden he bears, placed on your back,
Might cause you to stumble, too!

SATURDAY—MAY 7.

EVERYBODY who has anything to do with the Stock Exchange keeps in mind a little motto. It is: Never job backwards.

Having bought some shares at 59s 6d it is no use saying three weeks or four months later, " If only I'd bought them sooner (or later), I could have got them for 45s." Or, having sold some shares at a loss, it is no use a year afterwards grumbling, " It was a big mistake. I should have hung on to them a bit longer . . . I'd have made a packet !"

Talking or thinking in this way gets nobody anywhere in the buying or selling of shares. Hence: Never job backwards.

And what is pretty true of the share market is also true of life generally.

All you do when you sigh over the past is make yourself more miserable and less attractive to other people. If only you'd bought that little business . . . if only you'd written that letter home as you'd intended . . . if only you hadn't thrown up your job. Wishing things were different is a waste of time.

Don't do it.

SUNDAY—MAY 8.

EXCEPT the Lord build the house, they labour in vain that build it.

MONDAY—MAY 9.

FUNNY thing happened to me a short while ago. I had pain in my right leg, a bad pain.

That pain bothered me. I worried about it even when it subsided for a time. Too high blood pressure? Are you first aware of cancer when you have a nagging pain like that? Or most likely the prelude to a thrombosis? I said nothing to the Lady of the House—but I thought a lot. I may as well come clean—I was scared.

So I visited the doctor. He tested me. He said I was all right—and since then I have had no more of that pain!

TUESDAY—MAY 10.

I HEARD a service from Iona Abbey conducted by Dr George MacLeod. There was a great deal to ponder in all that Dr MacLeod said, but to me the most significant thing in the service came at the end, in the last words of the Benediction.

I expected to hear the blessing we all know—" The grace of our Lord Jesus Christ, the love of God, and the fellowship of the Holy Spirit, be with you all ..." But instead of saying " be with you all," Dr MacLeod said " is with you all."

In other words, he told us that no matter where we go or what we do, what we believe or what we worship—even if we spurn the name of God—His grace and love is still with us, whether we like it or not.

Remember that, my friend.

WEDNESDAY—MAY 11.

WHEN winter winds blow cold and strong—
  The fireside for me !
But summer days, so long and bright,
  Bring such sweet things to see
That I am all for venturing
  Mid golden fields outspread . . .
Now thank the Lord I'm well—and that
  I need not lie in bed !

THURSDAY—MAY 12.

MR STEVENSON, a friend of mine, is pretty well-to-do. Mr Stevenson is in his early fifties, owns a powerful car and has a hobby. He likes walking !

Not hiking. Mr Stevenson has quite a lot to say against hiking, one of his unkind comments being that it is too showy !

When Mr Stevenson walks he walks—just that, and only that. No special clothing. No pack on his back. No fuss. No grim determination on his face. As likely as not he takes a bus somewhere—five miles, or so, from his door, and steps down, waves a hand to the conductor, and just walks where fancy leads him, usually in pleasant country—perhaps along a not-too-busy lane or by a stream or over the moors. And he keeps on till he thinks it time to find another bus to take him home, or till he begins to feel tired.

And he will say—" Walking—just walking—has gone out of fashion, but it will come back. It keeps you fit if you don't overdo it. It gets you into lovely places. It expands your lungs. It tones your muscles. It gives you time to see the good things about you, and time to think. And, of course, it's nice getting back home !"

THINKING IT OUT

A hard-fought game, a sunny day,
  Each move considered at leisure;
What a pity the big chequerboard called Life
  Isn't played with the same youthful pleasure.

DAVID HOPE

" MY HOME "

Since Neil first built his castle
A thousand years have flown.
But Barra still holds vassal
The children of her own.

And far away, unknowing,
One day we hear the call,
And feel the west wind blowing
On Kismul's ancient wall.

DAVID HOPE

WHAT'S IT SAY?

First I meant to write to Mum,
Then I changed and did a sum.
You couldn't read it, I suppose.
But Mummy could!   She always knows.

DAVID HOPE

FRIDAY—MAY 13.

I OPENED the door. I said, "All being well I'll be home round about the usual time——"

" Stop !" commanded the Lady of the House,

So, dutifully and wonderingly, I stood still, the door half open.

Nothing much happened, however. The Lady of the House turned her back on me, opened her work-basket, threaded a needle, and then with a smile (but without my permission), cut a button off my jacket !

" Here, what's the big idea ?" I demanded.

" It was hanging loose," she explained, busy with her needle and thread. " It would have dropped off before the day was done. I'd much rather sew a button on before it comes off," said she.

It sounded nonsensical ... but you will know what she meant.

SATURDAY—MAY 14.

THE twins, aged three, were spending the afternoon with Grandpa. They'd been playing up rather more than usual—much too noisy and wilful, and far too inquisitive.

At last, during tea, the two naughty but fascinatingly pretty little girls went a step too far.

Grandpa knew his duty was clear, however difficult. So assuming a terrible aspect, his brows knit, his sharp eyes fixed relentlessly upon the diminutive guests, he commanded silence. Then, with an overwhelming show of importance, he began, " You two are the very naughtiest children——"

He got no further. A perky little voice piped up, " That ever you did see !"

Happily the mother of the twins arrived soon after that, and peace fell upon the house.

THE FRIENDSHIP BOOK

SUNDAY—MAY 15.

THE Lord upholdeth all that fall, and raiseth up all those that be bowed down.

MONDAY—MAY 16.

AS the years pile up it is easy to feel a bit bewildered and insecure—one never knows what tomorrow will bring—perhaps hardship, illness, loneliness, trouble. In youth and middle age one can keep on magnificently, but older folk have sometimes something very much like panic in their hearts.

A friend suggests that these lines may help:

Alone we falter day by day;
We take wrong turns or lose our way.
With God our steps are safe and sure,
Our path quite clear, our life secure.

TUESDAY—MAY 17.

THE Lady of the House and I saw the story of Field Marshal Montgomery on TV.

It was a thrilling programme. But the picture that remains with us is not of guns and tanks, or crashing enemy aircraft, or even of Monty's triumphant entry into Tunis.

Instead, we'll remember that moment at the end of the programme when Monty, speaking not as a soldier, but simply as a man who believes in God, took his Bible in his hands and read a verse of Scripture, telling us before he did so that his Bible is always by his bed, and that often he reads it just before he sleeps.

He has, in fact, found it to be the firmest foundation on which a man can build his life, whether he's a soldier or a sweep, a milkman or a millionaire, a dustman or a duke.

THE FRIENDSHIP BOOK

I WISH I had no end of things—a lot more cash to spend,
A finer house and heaps more time for chatting with a friend;
But where's the sense of sighing for the pleasures I have not
I cannot say how glad I am for all the things I've got !

THURSDAY—MAY 19.

I HAPPENED to be talking the other day with a young doctor who did brilliantly in all his medical exams and is likely to become a famous surgeon within a few years.

" What started it all ?" I asked. " Forgive me for mentioning it, but as a schoolboy you were not particularly bright. I remember that if you were halfway up the class there was astonishment at home."

The young doctor grinned. " And how right you are," said he. " Except that I'm not sure I ever rose to such dizzy heights as halfway up . . . not till I was seventeen !"

" And why the change ?"

He shrugged his shoulders. " Oh," said he lightly, " just one of those things. I happened to be looking in a book for one thing, and came upon another . . . . a saying by a famous Frenchman—' What matters in learning is not to be taught, but to wake up.'

" I couldn't make head or tail of it. I asked my father. He explained . . . and somehow the penny dropped. I saw how all along I'd just sat dumb and let folk tell me. All at once I wanted to find out for myself . . . and after that, well, there was no holding me !"

FRIDAY—MAY 20.

ABOUT noon the Lady of the House slipped into her coat, and hurried down the road with a helping of hot chicken and veg. between two plates.

Perhaps you're thinking my wife had taken a square meal to a poor old soul, huddled over her bit of fire.

But you would be wrong. The Lady of the House went to see an elderly woman with far more money than we are ever likely to have, a woman living in a big house, but living there alone. Her need of something to eat was not because she is shockingly poor, but simply through a combination of circumstances . . . husband and son are dead; former friends are growing old, she will keep on living in the house she loves and she cannot get anybody to look after her.

I mention her because old age and frailty belong not only to the poor, but to those who have ample means but find themselves rather lost and helpless, dependent on neighbours, and perhaps a wee bit too independent, bless them !

SATURDAY—MAY 21.

I WAS busy in the garden when the boy from down the road leaned over the gate. " Mr Gay," he grinned, " two men walked into a cafe. One asked for spaghetti and the other asked for egg and chips. How did the waitress know they were sailors ?"

I pursed my lips and furrowed my brows. I scratched my chin. But I knew I was stumped again —and so did Andrew.

" Give up, Mr Gay ?" he grinned—and I confessed I was beaten. " 'S'easy," he said. " They were wearing naval uniform !" And off he dodged before I could throw my hoe at him.

THE FRIENDSHIP BOOK

THOU shalt fear the Lord thy God, and serve Him.

MARY, who left Britain some time ago to join her husband in the United States, wrote me a letter.

She says she has such a lot to be thankful for—good parents back home, a devoted husband, a wonderful flat with every modern gadget, no money troubles, and time to explore the big new world.

But a few days ago she came very near to tears.

She was in a big store. It was crowded. What a lot there was to see, and how exciting visiting that spot for the first time ever—till suddenly she realised that there was not one person in all the crowd she knew, nobody likely to pause and smile, and say, " Hello !" Writes Mary from Chicago: " I was more lonely in that store than I've ever been in my life."

Funny how little relatives, friends and neighbours mean to us till we haven't them !

THE minister had been urging his congregation to try to live a finer life.

His eloquent and challenging sermon impressed many; but after the service one member of the congregation, a fine old lady with a nimble mind, remarked—

" It's no use going on like that and getting all worked up. The Lord works slowly on us and perfects us bit by bit. You and I aren't what we want or ought to be, and at present we're not what we're going to be when we pass over, but thank the Lord we are not what we were."

THE FRIENDSHIP BOOK

WERE I to count them one by one,
  My worries and my woes,
I'd find my ills and spills far more
  Than anybody knows.
I'd rather count my lucky stars,
  Life's twinkling bits of fun;
And when I do, I'm telling you,
  The task is never done!

I CALL them the irrepressible Irvines, Dad, Mum, and the lively trio of daughters.

And one day not long ago they went thirty miles into the hills for a picnic. It was to be the picnic of the year—and when the Irvines do a thing, they do it in tip-top style.

What preparations! Dad got out the old car. Mum buttered bread. Daughter One made sure they had the sausages and the frying pan. Daughter Two saw to cakes and pastries. Daughter Three made sure they had the teapot and the cups—and the tea! Dad examined the spirit lamp and packed stuff in the boot, including rugs and deck-chairs, and so on . . . and away they went in the sunshine, and found a hollow in the hills, with water rippling over rocks, and nobody else in sight.

Nobody had a match!

No tea to drink. No sausages to eat! And then, to crown all, a sudden heavy shower. So the Irvines came home.

But don't worry about them. Don't be sorry for them. Though it rained among the hills, it was dry and sunny at home, where (finding some matches) they had the jolliest picnic ever in the garden!

And the sausages were delicious!

FRIDAY—MAY 27.

I DID a bit of writing while the Lady of the House was out visiting a friend—and I lost my pencil. I mean I misplaced it, somehow.

Couldn't find it anywhere—hunted among the papers on the table. Looked under the table. Remembered I'd been into the kitchen, and hunted there for five minutes. No pencil. Minutes went by, and still the search continued.

Anyhow, I found it in the end—in my waistcoat pocket !

Well, well ! We sometimes can't see things because they are too near. I wonder if that is why some of us have to go abroad before we know what a nice street we live in ?

SATURDAY—MAY 28.

WALKING and talking with a schoolboy is always refreshing, and I cannot say how much I enjoyed a stroll on the beach in company with a laddie who was anxious to talk.

He talked of many things. " I saw a film a week or two ago," he exclaimed, " an educational film, all about astronomy. Makes you think, you know.

" It said that if you could gather up all the sand from all the beaches in the world, you'd find there are more stars than grains ! That took a bit of swallowing. I've been to places where there are miles of sand at low water ... and just think what a lot of grains you can hold in your hand. And yet, in all the universe there are more worlds than ... " He shrugged his shoulders, and looked up at me helplessly.

I nodded. I didn't feel I could say anything; but I thought how glorious it is to have a sense of wonder.

THE FRIENDSHIP BOOK

SUNDAY—MAY 29.

SEEK ye first the kingdom of God, and His righteousness.

MONDAY—MAY 30.

WHEN a woman died recently, her sister said, " I'm not surprised the Lord has taken Nellie.

" I've been expecting it quite a time," she went on. " I've no first-hand knowledge of what goes on in heaven, but if it's anything up there as it is down here, I just don't know how the Lord's managed so long without our Nellie to run and fetch and carry, and lend a hand and take the children by happy surprise and polish the door knocker and cook tasty bits for invalids, and sit still and let worried folk tell her their troubles.

" I shouldn't wonder if she's rushed off her feet already—and she hasn't been there twenty-four hours yet ! "

TUESDAY—MAY 31.

AS a boy of twenty Isaac Watts came home from church one day and complained to his father that there seemed so few good hymns to sing.

" Do you think you can do better ? " his father asked—and, taking up the challenge, young Isaac went on to give us some of our best hymns, including " O God, our help in ages past," " When I survey the wondrous Cross," and " Jesus shall reign where'er the sun."

But I think among the finest is this simple hymn—

There is a land of pure delight,
Where saints immortal reign;
Infinite day excludes the night,
And pleasures banish pain.

THE BONUS

There's something about our little old shop,
*   Which in smart, modern stores you don't see;*
The secret is simple — there's always a smile,
*   And not for my money — for me!*

E

DAVID HOPE

SEA LORE

" You must be skilled as well as bold,
Learn to tie the knots that hold:
Store up talk of rips and tides,
Bays to seek when tempest rides —"
Thus, boylike, while he waits and yearns,
All unconsciously he learns.

DAVID HOPE

JUNE

NOW, why not give yourself a treat—
Don't you deserve some fun?
Just give yourself a thrill that warms
Your heart when day is done.
Buy something sweet and nice to eat,
And share your time and tea
With some lone body . . . you will feel
As happy as can be!

I ALWAYS feel richer for having spent a few minutes with John.

He is not young now, but I never see him without recalling the days nearly 30 years back when his life was made up of two things only, earning his living and ministering to his brother, Kenneth.

That ministry went on day and night for over ten years. Gradually the younger brother found it more difficult to walk. Then John pushed him around in a wheelchair. Then he carried him to bed. Then he sat by the bedside and was up a dozen or more times every night to adjust a pillow or try to alleviate the pain . . . day after day, night after night as Kenneth became increasingly helpless, his joy less, his suffering more.

John never wearied in well doing, always believing that God is good, there is love behind all pain, and a hereafter to which one might look forward.

When Kenneth died, the postman brought a card. It was from John.

I have never forgotten it. It conveyed a quiet Christian's indomitable faith. It read—*Kenneth walked again today.*

THE FRIENDSHIP BOOK

I LIKE the story of a boy who was sent to learn from Titian, the great Italian artist. The boy worked in his master's studio, but he was soon sent back home with the message, " The lad is wasting his time. He will never be anything else but a dauber."

Well, surely Titian knew what he was talking about ? Surely he, of all people, could spot a flicker of artistic ability if it was there ? Surely *his* summing-up of that useless lad was the right one ?

But the dauber was Tintoretto, now acknowledged to be one of the world's most amazing painters.

You never know, you know !

I DOUBT if there's a better-known statue in London than that of Eros in Piccadilly Circus.

Yet I'm sure not one person in a hundred could tell you the statue stands in memory of Lord Shaftesbury, a man whose kindness and compassion were matched only by his strong faith.

It seems that some people who had never seen Lord Shaftesbury were asked to meet him at a big railway station. " How shall we know him ?" they asked.

The answer they were given was challenging. " When you see a tall man getting off the train and helping somebody, that will be Lord Shaftesbury." And, sure enough, when the tall man got out of the carriage and came towards them, he was carrying his suitcase in one hand, and in the other, the three shabby bundles of a little old woman.

It's worth keeping in mind that the truly great are never so high they can't reach down with a helping hand for the humble.

THE FRIENDSHIP BOOK

YOUR Father knoweth what things ye have need of, before ye ask Him.

A GROUP of small children were sitting in rows on chairs in the kitchen. " We're playing at churches," one of them explained when Mum came in.

" In that case," Mum remarked, " the children in the second row have no business to be whispering and giggling."

" Oh," was the reply, " that's okay, Mum. They're the choir."

"GRANNIE," said Jackie, " you're getting old, aren't you? When you die, do you think you'll go to heaven ?"

" Yes, Jackie, I do, if I try to do what's right before then."

" And do you think you'll find Jesus there ?"

" I'm sure of it."

" Do you expect to die before I do ?"

" Certainly. It ought to be a long time before you die."

Jackie was doing a lot of thinking. Then— " Grannie, I'm going to try to be good, and I'd like to see Jesus. Miss Greene, at Sunday School, says He'll be there at the gate to meet me, but I'd be awful scared if there was just Him and me, and I wouldn't know what to say, so if you go to heaven first, Grannie, make sure you're at the gate when I come along."

" I'll be there, Jackie," Grannie promised.

THE FRIENDSHIP BOOK

HOW quickly pass the busy hours,
How fast the moments fly ;
Too swift, too swift, life's little day . . .
What shadows, you and I !
Then, if there's any fleeting joy,
If there's one bit of fun,
Let's drink the rich, red wine of life
Before our journey's done !

JAMES WALKER was a farmer in the Aberdeen-shire parish of Newmachar.

His roots were planted deep in the land he loved, for the farm of Monykebbocks had been his home for many a long year, and to him it was the bonniest spot on God's good earth. Indeed, he never wanted to leave it.

In a strange and remarkable way, he never will. When he passed away he was laid to his rest, not in the churchyard, but in the soil of his beloved farm.

It happens that in the middle of one of the fields of Monykebbocks is an ancient graveyard where no one has been buried for 70 years. James often paused to look at it, thinking what a peaceful place it was, and he told his family that when his time came, he would like to lie there.

Now his wish has come true. Slowly he was carried from the gate of the field, over the wide path cut through the hay, to his chosen resting-place. And there, with his friends and family around him, he was laid to rest amid the fields.

Under the wide and starry sky,
Dig the grave and let me lie . . .
This be the verse you grave for me;
" Here he lies where he longed to be . . ."

FRIDAY—JUNE 10.

A FRIEND had looked in, and was hurrying home—late.

"Must get along," he told me. Then, with a smile, he opened his heavy, old-fashioned silver watch and said—"Look!"

I looked. Inscribed there was the couplet—

Tis mine the passing hour to tell.
Tis thine to use it ill or well.

"Life's a challenge," my friend remarked . . . and off he went, leaving me pondering, for all of us have as many hours a day, but—as the watch says—it is for us to use them ill or well!

SATURDAY—JUNE 11.

GEORGE MATHESON was a blind boy who became one of our greatest ministers. He wrote the wonderful hymn "O Love That Wilt Not Let Me Go" in five inspired minutes in Innellan manse one June evening over 80 years ago.

Maybe you don't know that every summer little groups of holidaymakers find their way to the church there that now bears his name, and sing his hymn under a chancel window which depicts the Light of the World.

And the wonderful thing they remember is that, because of some property in the stained glass, the lantern in our Saviour's hand glows warmly on the dullest day.

Dr Matheson ministered for 18 years beneath that same window, yet he could not see it.

But who knows how many have been uplifted —and are still uplifted—by the glowing lamp of Innellan, and a faith that shone out of darkness like a beacon?

THE FRIENDSHIP BOOK

SUNDAY—JUNE 12.

WHEN thou doest alms, let not thy left hand know what thy right hand doeth.

MONDAY—JUNE 13.

WHEN somebody asked Paderewski the secret of his amazing skill as a pianist, he hesitated quite a while before replying.

At last he said—" I am not sure. I expect music was born in me. If I can take any credit at all for being able to play the piano it is perhaps because every day I practise scales for hours."

" Scales?" repeated his admirer. " Just scales?" Paderewski nodded. " Scales," said he, smiling. " If I cannot do the simple things easily and without thinking, how am I to do the harder ones?"

I rather think quite a lot of people bungle living because they are too eager to do big things, attract attention, win popularity or honours instead of trying to do a lot of ordinary little things and quite unspectacular kindnesses as and when they can. It's nice to give a thousand pounds to a charity . . . but it's a pity not to lend a helping hand when someone needs it.

TUESDAY—JUNE 14.

A FRIEND handed me this verse, saying it had given him food for more than a passing thought:—
In the Church's field of battle,
In her labour and her strife,
You will find the Christian soldier
Represented by his wife!
Am I right in thinking that these four lines sum up the reason for a good deal of the Church's failure—and also, perhaps, much of its success?

WEDNESDAY—JUNE 15.

*D*EPEND *upon it, if you look for things you
    must deplore,*
*You'll find so much is wrong, you'll start to grumble
    more and more ;*
But also, it is very true that if, with spirit gay,
*You seek the best, you'll smile along and find it every
    day !*

THURSDAY—JUNE 16.

*N*EARLY 120 years ago, in a London house, a
    little boy lay dying.

He was a victim of diphtheria, and, although
everything had been done to save him, it had been
in vain.

As his parents, brokenhearted, waited by his
bed for the end they knew must come, the doctor
rose from his chair and bent over the boy. When
he looked up, the father knew it was all over.
Gently, he led the weeping mother away.

That night the undertaker arrived. But, in the
midst of the funeral arrangements, he stopped in
amazement—for surely the child still lived ! Sure
enough, when he put his ear to the boy's breast he
heard the faintest of heartbeats—and when the
doctor was called, he told the father and mother
that their son was going to get better.

The little boy did, in fact, survive, and what a
blessing it was that he did. For his name was
Thomas John Barnardo, and he grew up to be the
famous founder of Dr Barnardo's Homes, the man
who rescued homeless and orphan children.

Today, Dr Barnardo's task still goes on. How
proud he would be of his boys and girls, for I know
they become some of the finest men and women
of our day.

THE FRIENDSHIP BOOK

DID you hear about the boy, aged four, and blessed with a gloriously disarming smile?

Wandering happily into the village store recently, he asked the little lady there—" How much will a pennyworth of sweets cost?"

The proprietor of the shop chuckled inwardly, but managed to keep a straight face. Into a paper bag she popped sweets to the value of sixpence, at least, handed them to the cute little customer, and said—" There you are, sonny. And there's your penny back!"

She laughed again as she watched him go. But the customer was thinking. At the door he turned. Again that lovely smile. Then—" I think I'll have another pennyworth please!"

I WALKED home alone in the darkness with my thoughts.

I was thinking about Jean, who a few years ago was so pretty and lively, and who is now flat on her back, slowly wasting away.

And as often before, I was thinking about John her husband—still youngish, devoted, brave as a lion, cracking jokes in the bedroom, staying at home seven nights a week.

And I wondered which of this couple needed the most sympathy—the patient who knows she is dying or the husband who is fighting a losing battle so gallantly.

There in the darkness I prayed that God would bless and comfort these two . . . and I wondered how many men and women there are, watching by beds of suffering, themselves suffering as acutely (perhaps even more so) than those who are ill.

SUNDAY—JUNE 19.

WHOSOEVER shall compel thee to go a mile, go with him twain.

MONDAY—JUNE 20.

DON'T miss it. Don't let it slip by. Don't be so busy that you never notice it.

In the cold, dull days of winter this is the time you longed for and thought about—high summer, the best and the pride of the year. June which brings the roses under blue skies (sometimes, at any rate), and gives the outdoor world a glory and magic which comes quickly upon us and passes all too soon.

Whatever else you have to do, however busy you may be, don't miss the sunny evenings if you can possibly enjoy them. Don't let the colour in the gardens or the greenness of the countryside pass its zenith before you wake up to the fact that summer is here . . . and summer is passing, quickly, quickly.

Don't miss it!

TUESDAY—JUNE 21.

TODAY is the longest day.

A long day, indeed, and, just for one moment during it, I want you to do something for me. It won't be difficult, for all I ask you to do is to give a thought for the mothers of this world. Surely for them more than anyone else, every day is a long day, of constant care and thought and unselfishness and . . . I could go on for ever, couldn't I?

There's an old, old legend which says that when God made the world He knew He'd be very busy looking after it, so He made mothers to help Him.

And how faithful they are to that trust.

WEDNESDAY—JUNE 22.

*I*T seems a little odd to me that folk whose needs are few
And live in comfort may complain they've far too much to do.
A little odd that often those with spirits gay enough
Are just those smiling, cheery folk for whom the going's tough!

THURSDAY—JUNE 23.

IF you ever happen to be walking in Dundee, pause by the notice-board outside St John's Church.

At the top of the board, carved in wood, are these words—" The Master is come, and calleth for thee."

It seems a member of the congregation had been stricken by an illness which made him a semi-invalid. Much of his life was spent in bed, but he was a man of strong faith, and his Bible was never far from his side. Then, one day, his wife went up to the room where he lay, and found that the end had come swiftly and unexpectedly.

Yet the strange thing is he may have known the end was near, for his Bible lay open by his side, at the eleventh chapter of St John, and his hand rested near the verse which reads—" The Master is come, and calleth for thee . . ."

It was almost as if, sudden though his passing was, he had been prepared for the step into the unknown.

In the dark days that followed, these same words gave his wife the strength to go on, and that is why she had them carved on the notice-board she erected at her church—a constant challenge to all who pass by.

THE FRIENDSHIP BOOK

HOW old are you ? Sorry if I seem rude. But I'm not thinking specially of your physical age.

I'm thinking of the way you look at life. You may not be thirty, and yet be very old ... much too solemn and serious, far too cautious and a great deal more concerned with your health than you have any right to be.

And you may have touched sixty or seventy and yet have a quick mind, a cheery spirit, a genius for adapting yourself to changing conditions—which is another way of saying you are still wonderfully young.

I suggest it's your duty now and then to ask yourself how old you are ... and whether or not you could be a lot younger if you tried !

I WISH we could all peep through the door of any ward in Leeds Infirmary any morning at half-past seven.

Instead of bustling about their morning tasks, the nurses are kneeling round the table in the centre of each ward, praying for their patients.

The matron tells me it has become a kind of tradition in the hospital and that it has been carried on for many years. Just before the night nurses go off duty and as the day nurses take over, they kneel together in this quiet communion, and led by the sister, they ask God to bless the folk in their care and to help them in their work of healing.

In this way, every nurse in all 39 wards remembers her patients every morning, and I am sure it is a comfort to the sick and anxious folk who lie waiting and wondering, to know they are in the care of girls like these.

SUNDAY—JUNE 26.

BLESSED are they that mourn : for they shall be comforted.

MONDAY—JUNE 27.

ACCORDING to the story, a young man declared to his beloved that he loved her more than tongue could tell; that for her he would gladly lay down his life; that he would swim vast oceans or climb the steepest mountains . . . and so on.

But the young lady, it seems, was a little less poetic and a bit more practical. " Jimmy," said she, " when we're married, will you get up first and make a cup of tea ?"

Of course, she was right—because real love is not passion or making brave promises . . . it is serving all the time.

TUESDAY—JUNE 28.

A NEWSPAPER man was sent to interview a little lady on her 99th birthday.

Of course he took a snap of her—and of the cake. Of course he asked many questions. Of course he asked the one question all reporters ask on such occasions, " What's your secret ? How have you managed to live ninety-nine years ?"

The reply was, I think, priceless and also challenging. " Why," said the old lady, " by living a day at a time."

She was not as simple as you might think. After all, no end of people die long before ninety-nine because they worry themselves into their graves, carry tomorrow's burden today, plan anxiously ahead . . . doing anything, anything except living a day at a time.

THE FRIENDSHIP BOOK

YOU'VE reached the end, you think, my friend,
All hope, all strength is gone ;
But if you pray you'll find a way—
To keep on keeping on !

THIS story, I hear, was told not long ago by the Archbishop of Paris in the great cathedral of Notre Dame.

Many years before, he said, three youths had entered that very cathedral, scornful of all it stood for. They noticed a priest hearing confession, and two of them bet the other he would not approach the priest and give a false confession.

The young man accepted the bet, but the priest realised what was happening. He waited in silence until the youth stopped speaking, then he told him that for every confession there must be penance made. " Your penance," he said, " is to go to the high altar, kneel before the great golden cross there, and say to it three times, ' All this you did for me— and I don't give a damn !' "

The young man wished then he had never started out on his prank, but his friends kept him to his word. Hesitantly he approached the cross and sank to his knees. In a whisper he began to repeat the words the priest had bade him speak. But so full of shame was he, he could say them only once. Indeed, his words of penance became a prayer for forgiveness, and he rose a changed person.

That is the story the Archbishop told—but it is only half the story. For after a moment's pause he said simply, " My friends, the youth who knelt at the cross that day is the man who is speaking to you now."

JULY

PSYCHOLOGISTS say that mind rules matter, and what we are depends on how we think.

There's something in it. Hence the little rhyme sent to me by a friend who suffered a good deal till she visited her doctor:—

> When I am ill I take a pill,
> And it is understood
> That I must tell myself this pill
> Is going to do me good.

And it does !

THIS fine story concerns a young man at college, training to be a missionary.

Above his bed was a hand-lettered sign which bore three words—" I am third." When a friend asked him what it meant, the young man shook his head. " Ask me again sometime," he said—and changed the subject.

But the sign stayed there all through his college years, and on the day he graduated, his friend came to help him pack his books and clothing and to see him off at the station. Just before the train left for the north, he asked again what the words meant.

The young man hesitated. Then, quietly he told how, when he had left home, his mother had told him to remember always that God came first, others second, and he came third. To help him to carry out her advice, he made the little sign, and put it where he would see it every day.

So he obeyed it all through his college days, and he followed its teaching through his life until he died of fever serving lepers in Africa.

SUNDAY—JULY 3.

WHOSOEVER heareth these sayings of mine, and doeth them, I will liken them unto a wise man, which built his house upon a rock.

MONDAY—JULY 4.

DO you know your geography?

If so, maybe you can answer the question a laddie asked me the other day:—

" Mr Gay," he purred, " you're a smart guy. I fancy you will know where the finest songs are sung and the greatest applause given? It's the place where brilliantly witty speeches are made, and where sometimes orators rise to dizzy heights, always bringing down the house, of course. You'll know where it is, sure."

I was stroking my chin.

" Just to help a bit," the lad went on, " I'll tell you that in the same place great business deals are pulled off, and even Olympic gold medals are won."

I shrugged my shoulders. " Give it up," I said.

The laddie grinned. His answer was one word— " Bed !"

TUESDAY—JULY 5.

WHAT happens to you is of less importance than how you take it.

If something hits you hard you can wail and lie down, or you can stand up to it, put a smile on, and make the best of it. The latter is always the hard thing to do, and always the best in the end.

I'm thinking of a word of wisdom from that great humorist, Josh Billings. He preached a sermon in only 13 words—" The best medicine I know for rheumatism's thanking the Lord it ain't gout."

WEDNESDAY—JULY 6.

> A LITTLE *bit less of* " *I'll get,*"
>   *A little bit more of* " *I'll give.*"
> *Less getting, more giving—that way*
>   *You grow richer and richer each day.*

THURSDAY—JULY 7.

COME back with me in time to an orphanage in London more than a hundred years ago . . .

A little band of homeless children are sitting by the fire, waiting to go to bed. Suddenly the door of the room opens and in walks a man with a kindly face and a gentle smile. With shouts of glee the children rush to meet him, and soon he is seated in their midst, telling them a story while they listen, wide eyed and silent.

It is a happy scene, and one that was repeated again and again, for never a week went by without a call from the friendly visitor, and the children grew to love him.

He was James Edmeston, a gifted London architect, and, though he could have spent his time among great men, he preferred the company of these little children.

It was there, in the orphanage, he found the inspiration that led him to write one of our loveliest hymns, dedicated to the children, and if you read it you will see how deeply he understood and felt for them:—

> *Lead us, heavenly Father, lead us,*
>   *O'er the world's tempestuous sea;*
> *Guard us, guide us, keep us, feed us,*
>   *For we have no help but Thee* . . .

Of course, James has been dead for a long time now—but his simple prayer will rise to heaven for countless years to come.

THE PATH

Everyone has known a path like this;
   Has walked it on a perfect summer day.
Everyone has known its timeless bliss;
   The country air, the scent of fresh-mown hay.

It is the path which leads to years gone by;
   To places where we once had time to roam.
To old church towers, to golden days that fly,
   To memories, and—most of all—to home.

DAVID HOPE

BEAUTY

How can we measure loveliness?
   By form, or width, or height?
Enough that to this darkling world
   It brings a little light.

DAVID HOPE

FRIDAY—JULY 8.

I HAVE always known it as the Clydeside Prayer.
Whether or not it was in actual fact first uttered
in Clydeside years ago when no end of folk were
out of work and most homes were overshadowed
by poverty I could not say. The story is that it
was a girl who first used the words.

For anything I know, there may still be devout
churchfolk who will be shocked by such an uncon-
ventional prayer; but I feel it springs from a desperate sense of need and a complete belief in the
goodness of God:—

*Dear God, take care of yourself, for without You
we are sunk.*

SATURDAY—JULY 9.

SOME months ago a commercial traveller came
across a few lines which have lived with him
ever since.

Often driving from one shop to another—and
with nobody to talk to—he sings a little verse
which does him a world of good. This is the verse:—

You've got to have the goods, my boy,
  If you would finish strong.
A bluff may work a little while—
  But not for very long.
A line of talk all by itself
  Will seldom see you through.
You've *got* to have the goods, my boy,
  And nothing else will do.

And, depend on it, this does not apply only to
commercial travellers—in life generally you can
persuade with cunning, you can pull strings galore
—but the only sure way to happiness and success
depends finally on whether or not you deliver the
goods!

SUNDAY—JULY 10.

TRUST in the Lord with all thine heart; and lean not unto thine own understanding.

MONDAY—JULY 11.

VERY often I spend the last half-hour of the day browsing in Dean Ramsay's "Reminiscences of Scottish Life and Character." It always sends me to bed with a chuckle.

My favourite story is the one about John Clerk, who later became Lord Eldin, the judge.

John, it seems, was arguing a Scottish appeal case before the House of Lords. He had occasion to keep referring, in broad Scots, to the watter in a stream which ran by a mill.

He mentioned the watter so often that the Chancellor, amused by the pronunciation of the Scottish advocate, asked banteringly, "Mr Clerk, do you spell water in Scotland with two t's?"

John Clerk, nettled by this jibe at his national tongue, retorted, "No, my lord, we dinna spell watter wi' twa t's, but we spell manners wi' twa n's."

TUESDAY—JULY 12.

I CANNOT help feeling there is a moral somewhere in this story:—

Dad was speaking severely to his schoolboy son, and when the lecture was over the little fellow looked up and asked, "Dad, didn't you ever eat apples in school when you were my age, or scamp your homework because you had something really important to do?"

My heart bleeds for Dad.

What could he say in reply, with that schoolboy's granny sitting close by?

THE FRIENDSHIP BOOK

*THE other day, while at the sink, I saw the morning
  sun,
A singing stream and hawthorn white, and, oh,
  what childish fun !
I skipped with Arabella Jane and with my cousin
  Joe . . .
I saw it all—as clear and bright as 60 years ago !*

I FEEL like ordering a 21-gun salute for the sailor
  with the spade !

He's Chief Petty Officer John Barlow, of H.M.S.
Condor, Arbroath. John, who comes from Ipswich,
being a friendly sort of man, began to wonder what
he could do to repay the folk of Arbroath for the
kindness they showed him.

As he went through the town he noticed several
old folk had gardens that were getting a bit much
for them. So he decided he would look after their
gardens for them—and he has been doing it ever
since.

Now, you might think that digging a garden is as
far removed as you can get from a life on the ocean
wave, but that doesn't worry John. Without being
asked, he regularly turns up at half a dozen gardens
in his spare time, to dig, hoe, rake, and mow. I'm
told he also buys seeds and plants, and carefully
looks after them, so that when spring and summer
come along the old folk have a fine show of flowers
to look at.

I hear that when John leaves the navy he's
hoping to stay on in Arbroath, for he'd be sorry to
leave. I know I'm speaking for all his pensioner
friends when I say they'd be even sorrier to see him
go—for the smiling sailor has won their hearts.

FRIDAY—JULY 15.

THEY were a wonderful couple.

They were devoted to each other, faced life bravely, and made a good thing of it till the wife was overcome by a brain disorder. With the help of a neighbour, the husband cared for her till the day came when he himself was crippled by a disease—and the good neighbour died. Now the wife is in a mental home, the husband in a home for incurables.

Now and again I think it is wise to record something which is likely to depress rather than comfort and cheer. For only in this way can I remind you that even in these days when doctors can do so much, there is terrible suffering and there are still thousands of folk finding each day cruel and wretched.

It is good for us sometimes to face these facts, and be all the more ready to share others' burdens as and when we can.

SATURDAY—JULY 16.

FRANKLY, I would have preferred walking home that fine afternoon, but when a professor of psychology invites you into his car, what can you do ? So in I got, and thanked him—and felt I must ask some sensible question. " And when," I ventured, " do you think a man is happiest ?"

I expected a reply far beyond my comprehension —something to do with complexes and inhibitions, motivations, and so on, but the psychologist grinned, looked at me with curiously schoolboyish eyes, and said, " When he's rushed off his feet and tired out and fifty things to do."

I called him a nitwit, thanked him for the lift— and began wondering if, after all, he is right.

SUNDAY—JULY 17.

AS a man chasteneth his son, so the Lord thy God chasteneth thee.

MONDAY—JULY 18.

LORD, for sunshine and fresh breezes, for mountains to climb and seas to sail on, for hard work and the luxury of holidays, for trees and flowers and birds, for new scenes and dear, familiar places, for the pleasures of food and drink, for books and pictures and sports and pastimes, and for the delight of sitting and nodding off to sleep and the joy of being active, for home and family and friends and surprises and colour and movement and music and memories of yesterday and hopes for tomorrow, for day with its wonder and night and its rest we thank Thee, Lord.

TUESDAY—JULY 19.

AN Englishman went abroad for the first time. He was determined to see all he could, and to keep a journal of his travels.

Leaving Dover, this careful observer made notes as to the condition of the sea, the direction of the wind, and so forth, all with meticulous attention to detail; and as they tied up at Calais—his first glimpse of Europe—he caught sight of a deformed porter on the quay. Out came his newly begun journal, and in it the acute observer recorded, " The French are a hunchback race."

How ridiculous of him to generalise from a single particular ! What a stupid fellow he was.

I agree, and heartily.

But at the same time I must take care that I do not get a twist in my thinking.

WEDNESDAY—JULY 20.

I'VE never met a perfect saint—
The best of us fall short.
I've never met a villain who
Had not one kindly thought.

So I am slow to pick upon
The faults I find in others,
And try to see what good there is
In all my erring brothers!

THURSDAY—JULY 21.

AN old woman went to her minister with a strange and moving request.

It was this—that very day she had moved house. It wasn't much, just a wee home up two stairs in a tenement. But it was her home, and now she wanted her minister to come and bless it.

It was a lovely thought, wasn't it? Of course, the minister was honoured to do as she asked, and he told her so. So next day he climbed the steps up to her door and was welcomed into the house. Then in the kitchen, amid all the treasured things she had brought with her, the old lady knelt with her minister on the rug before the fire.

The minister asked God's blessing on the humble home, that it might be a place where peace and love would abound. He prayed, too, for the old soul by his side, that she might find happiness and peace in it.

Soon it was over and the minister went off on his rounds again. Yet, for me at least, this little act of consecration has given a new meaning to a grand old song:—

Bless this house, O Lord, we pray,
Make it safe by night and day . . .

FRIDAY—JULY 22.

SOMEBODY was singing softly in the garden the other evening. I listened, but couldn't catch the words though I liked the catchy tune.

I crossed the lawn and looked down at the Lady of the House, who was busy with a trowel. " Sing it a bit louder," I commanded.

" Tut, tut," said she, " what a way to speak to a lady !" Having waved the trowel menacingly, she smiled. " Heard it on TV weeks ago," said she. " Liked the tune. Think the words ought to be repeated three times before breakfast by everybody."

Then, beating time with the trowel, she sang, still softly so as not to annoy the neighbours (as she put it)—

" *As you go through life let this be your goal:*
Look for the doughnut—not the hole !"

SATURDAY—JULY 23.

I HAVE a friend in Canada who likes passing on funny stories. Here are two he sent me the other day:—

First, the tale of the man who complained that he and his wife had no home. " Well," remarked an acquaintance, " why don't you live with your mother and father till you get somewhere of your own ?"

" I can't !" wailed the homeless one. " That's what my mother and father are doing !"

And the other story. When the husband, seeing a bus departing, exclaimed, " There it goes ! If only you'd hurried a bit we should have caught it."

His wife tossed her head angrily. " If only you hadn't hurried me so much," she snapped, " we shouldn't have so long to wait for the next bus !"

SUNDAY—JULY 24.

GIVE unto the Lord the glory due unto His name.

MONDAY—JULY 25.

"OVER and over again," said Mrs Waterworth to the Lady of the House, " I get sick and fed up with housework—all the chores and the regular daily round and shopping and washing up— and I wish I could down tools and have a week at Blackpool or Bournemouth or Scarborough."

Mrs Waterworth sighed. Then she added, " And time and time again we have gone to Blackpool or Bournemouth or Scarborough for a week—and, believe you me, after the first day or two I find myself just longing to be back running my home, seeing to things—back at the same old grind you know! Queer!"

TUESDAY—JULY 26.

THE biggest cause of trouble is want of thought. So said a wise man long, long ago.

Whether or not he is altogether right I cannot say—I am not wise enough—but that mostly he is right there is no denying.

When I consider some of the thousands of letters which reach me every year I realise over and over again that people are in debt, out of work, at odds with their families, suffering in body or mind, lonely or too busy not because they themselves are particularly bad or blameworthy, not because those about them are near-criminal—but just because so many folk will not think a little more, consider, weigh things up.

Whatever you intend doing tomorrow, think about it today.

THE WAYS OF NATURE

Nothing in nature is wasted
  With so many creatures to feed;
When this poppy's petals have fallen
  It leaves a rich banquet of seed!

F

DAVID HOPE

THE PATTERN

There's a pattern to life, never doubt it,
There's a way through its intricate maze.
Though cause and effect may elude you,
There's a pattern through all of our days.

It's a pattern that's carefully blended
From sorrow, joy, pleasure and pain.
As we don't get all tears and no laughter
So — we don't get all sun and no rain.

DAVID HOPE

QUIET MOMENTS

The little things, the simple things,
The fleeting, half-forgotten things—
So seldom contemplated.
The precious things, remembered things,
The secret, sad and silent things—
Of such is Life created.

DAVID HOPE

THE FRIENDSHIP BOOK

UP the steep road with my burden,
Up to the kirk on the hill;
There will I pray and will listen,
There God and I will be still.
Panting and groaning I toil up,
Weary with trouble and pain;
Strong and refreshed in my spirit,
Singing, I come down again.

THE holiday season is in full swing. So it may not be amiss to suggest ten commandments for holidaymakers—

Thou shalt not treat waiters, waitresses, chambermaids, bus conductors, landladies, and foreigners as inferior beings.

Thou shalt not become another bore in the hotel lounge.

Remember the folk at home that the days of thy pleasure may be fruitful.

Thou shalt take thine own sunshine with thee and leave a grumbling spirit behind.

Thou shalt not forget thy good manners, even in a far country.

Thou shalt not steal another holidaymaker's pitch on the sand, neither his place in the theatre queue, nor his bit of peace nor anything that is his.

Thou shalt make time to be still and meditate.

Thou shalt not leave behind thee litter in streets, parks or open spaces, neither shalt thou enjoy thyself so loudly that nobody else can.

Thou shalt not pretend to be more important than thou art.

And, for goodness sake, shut up sometimes, and listen !

FRIDAY—JULY 29.

WHAT a lot is wrong in these days.

Standards have been lowered in the last 20 years or so, discontent seems to be all around, and everywhere there are indications that men and women have fallen away from the ideals cherished by their forebears.

I am with those who are sorry about all this.

But I believe these days are a challenge to those of us who still believe in God—a challenge to be loyal to our faith, to keep our churches, to witness quietly but courageously to what we believe, and thus to prepare for that wind of change which will surely blow one day, the day when millions will learn afresh that there is only one way to live, and that is according to God's Word.

SATURDAY—JULY 30.

AS far as I know I never met Mr William Crawford.

He lived in Yorkshire, and was for 20 years a councillor in the small town of Driffield. Although these are all the facts I know about him, I feel I have a very good idea of the kind of man he was.

He was selfless. He went about doing good quietly. He had a strong but simple faith, and was never afraid of declaring what he believed.

How can I be sure I am right about Mr Crawford? The answer is that after his death a card was found in his wallet. It read:—

Think fairly. Love widely. Witness humbly. Build bravely.

SUNDAY—JULY 31.

KEEP the commandments of the Lord thy God, to walk in His ways, and to fear Him.

AUGUST

THE late Dr Johnstone Jeffrey used to tell this little story of the First World War—

One day he met a private who had just arrived from France and stood chatting with him at a street corner. The young soldier was carrying a load which seemed almost too much even for a big, healthy lad, and the doctor wondered how he could trudge along in such heavy boots with so much on his shoulders.

' By the way," said Dr Jeffrey, " how far can you march with all that ?"

The boy replied promptly, " Oh, about twelve miles, sir." Then, as an afterthought, he added— " But fifteen with a band !"

And I rather imagine that men and women, weighed down with work and worry and travelling a hard road, can go farther and endure more if a bit of faith enables them to keep a song in their heart.

Tuesday—August 2.

" HOOLIGANS don't come from happy homes," said a woman in the bus.

Certainly it was a bold assertion. But, the more I think about it, the more convinced I am there is a lot of truth in it. I cannot help feeling that children who know they are loved, whose parents take an interest in their doings and who find home a place where understanding abounds—these children *may* grow up to be hooligans, but it's not likely.

I remember an old lady telling me years ago, " You can spank your children too much. You can neglect them too much. You can preach to them too much ... but you can never love them too much."

WEDNESDAY—AUGUST 3.

*SAY, what a thrill to pack your bags and
start on holiday.
What fun to leave the daily round and
travel miles away !
There's nothing I love better than untrodden
paths to roam,
Except, of course, that greater thrill—the
thrill of coming home !*

THURSDAY—AUGUST 4.

SOME of us find the going pretty rough and rather
hectic.

Life is not all that easy for most of us. It can be
very trying at times.

If you are bewildered or anxious or troubled
in mind and spirit or frustrated or bitterly disappointed, I suggest this thought—

*Prayer is the key of the morning and
the lock of the door at night.*

FRIDAY—AUGUST 5.

HERE are a few more ten-second sermons that
are worth more than ten seconds' thought—

*We make a living by what we get—but we make a
life by what we give.*

Faith is a steering wheel—not a spare wheel.

*A good sermon helps in two ways—some rise from
it strengthened, others wake from it refreshed !*

*If you're not so close to God as you once were,
don't be mistaken about who's moved.*

*Married folk should remember that in " wedding "
the " we " comes before the " I."*

*The steam that does the work is invisible. It's the
waste that makes all the fuss.*

SATURDAY—AUGUST 6.

THE Lady of the House and I visited Glamis Castle. We were led up the winding stone stair into rooms filled with priceless pictures and furniture; we saw the Queen Mother's own splendid rooms, suits of armour centuries old, great open fireplaces, and round it all, like a great colourful tapestry, was woven the ancient history of Glamis, with it's stirring tales of long ago.

As we left the castle and stepped out into the sunshine, I was still spell-bound by the past that had been unfolded before our eyes. Then the Lady of the House turned to me, and do you know what she said ? " Really, Francis, we'll have to do something about that back kitchen of ours. It's been an eyesore for years."

How like a woman.

SUNDAY—AUGUST 7.

SEEK the Lord and His strength, seek His face continually.

MONDAY—AUGUST 8.

AN old lady happened to be seated in church beside a wee boy. When the time came for the collection to be taken, the old body began fumbling through her purse and, oh calamity, found she'd come away without any money !

But the young gentleman of five sitting next her took command of the situation. With a swift glance to ensure no one was watching, he nudged her elbow. " Here, missus," he whispered, " you take my penny. I can hide under the seat !"

That, men, is what the Lady of the House would term the height of chivalry !

THE FRIENDSHIP BOOK

TUESDAY—AUGUST 9.

THE other day, I spent an hour in a Salvation Army eventide home, chatting to the old folk.

Our talk turned to hymns, and I asked them which, of all their favourites, was the one they liked above all others. I expected the answer might be " Abide with me " or " Lead, kindly light."

But I was wrong! I found the favourite of the old folk is the rousing song, " Count your blessings." It may seem a strange choice, for I'm sure no one could say that, by this world's standards, any of the old folk in the eventide home have been richly blessed. Yet, if you hear their voices raised in the spirited singing of this fine old hymn, you would know they mean every word of it.

As I listened to them, I remembered how, years ago, I had been deeply moved by the same hymn. I stood then in a tiny gallery of the chapel of Quarrier's Homes at Bridge of Weir, gazing down on row upon row of orphan boys and girls, listening as their fresh, young voices sang " Count your blessings, name them one by one." It was an experience I have never forgotten.

Can it be, I wonder, that the more we have, the less thankful we tend to become—and that it takes an orphan or an old body to shame us into realising how blind we are to our blessings?

WEDNESDAY—AUGUST 10.

A BUDDY with a garden grows lettuce,
  bean and pea,
And cucumber and eschalot as tasty as can be.
I never eat this expert's stuff without a thrill
  . . . you see,
The man who grows these scrumptious things
  (as my wife knows) is me!

THURSDAY—AUGUST 11.

I WALKED a little way in step with the minister after the evening service, and he surprised me by saying, " I omitted one point in my sermon. I didn't mention one of our greatest and most common sins."

I thought quite a time. Then I asked, " What's that ?"

The minister smiled. " Being too busy," he said. " It's a common fault. It's yours, Mr Gay, and mine. So often we are too busy and noisy to hear God speak, too bothered about our own troubles to understand other people's. We need," went on the minister, quoting a famous hymn, " a heart at leisure from itself to soothe and sympathise."

Could I do anything other than agree ?

FRIDAY—AUGUST 12.

THE other day I met a friend, an accountant, who told me he had been doing the books for a nunnery.

" Frankly," he admitted, " I wasn't keen on the task—but I needn't have worried. They installed me in their beautiful library. They supplied me with tea and biscuits, and provided a delicious lunch. They chatted with me, and asked after my family —they were, bless them, kindness itself, and so full of fun !"

Then he added—" But, really, the oddest thing of all was the opening of the library door one afternoon, and in came a very, very little nun. She spoke no word. She went straight to a shelf, tugged out an enormous volume, and made off on tiptoe. ' You're going to do some hard studying,' I said.

" She chuckled. ' I'm not,' said she. ' It's to sit on !' "

SATURDAY—AUGUST 13.

MANY a time I've written of the Lady of the House sitting by the fire—curled up in the armchair. But have I told you about her thinking chair?

Now and again she sits in a little rocking chair, and, when she does — rocking to and fro, knitting needles flashing — I know she is steadily, persistently and cautiously thinking through a problem.

At such times I nod, settle myself in my chair, and ask no questions. Sometimes, bless her soul, she'll sit half an hour, maybe even an hour—knitting without looking at her needles, staring into space, rocking gently to and fro till at last she smiles, and says, " There now, that's settled !"

And settled it is, without the least effort on the part of yours truly.

There's a lot to be said for rocking chairs !

SUNDAY—AUGUST 14.

BLESSED are the merciful : for they shall obtain mercy.

MONDAY—AUGUST 15.

AN amazing thing about this old world is that it never grows old !

It cannot—not as long as there are children in it, anyhow. Bless them, they have refreshing thoughts that keep us on our toes.

I am thinking of wee Peter.

" Eat up your sago pudding," Mum coaxed one dinner-time. As her son seemed reluctant to obey, she added—" Just think, dear, thousands of little boys would be glad to have some nice sago pudding."

Retorted Peter promptly. " Come on, Mum, name just one, and let's have a bet on it !"

THE LORDLY ONES

Where winds blow fresh and water flows
And peaks spring undefiled,
In grace and strength he proudly goes,
True spirit of the wild.

G

DAVID HOPE

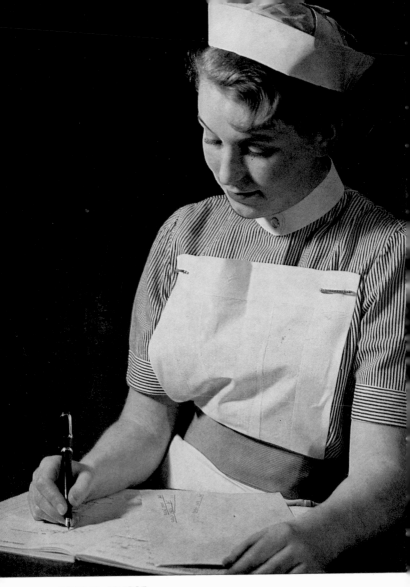

NIGHT NURSE

When restless in our pain we face
The night's long load of care,
Our thanks unuttered flow to her
For simply being there.

DAVID HOPE

THE FRIENDSHIP BOOK

THIS is the story of the two pensions.

I'm thinking of the daughter of a couple who both died from cancer.

Fortunately, although the daughter's grief was great and she was left alone in the world, she had her parents' home to live in and a steady job, with a pension. So, as all of us must do in our time, she gradually overcame her pain and learned to face the world again.

She never married. She found her happiness in her work and her home—and in a secret task to which she dedicated herself for the rest of her life, and which was discovered only the other day.

For it was then, after she, too, had died, that the British Empire Cancer Campaign, received from her agents a cheque for £1900 to aid cancer research. Yes, £1900—and every penny of it she had earned.

You see, the money was her entire pension from her job, from the day she retired to the day she died. She saved it all, and used her old-age pension for her day-to-day needs.

It was her own way of helping in the battle to find a cure for the disease which robbed her of her beloved mother and father.

EVERYBODY'S going away—
So, at least, it seems;
Only me a-sitting here,
Dreaming pleasant dreams . . .
Hoping folk on holiday
Are happy as can be—
Lovely if, when they return,
They share their fun with me !

THURSDAY—AUGUST 18.

MRS THOMSON'S grandson, aged five, was in a thoughtful mood. Apparently the little chap had noticed, perhaps for the first time, that his grandmother is much smaller than his mother. "Gran," said he, "what will you do when you grow up?"

Grannie had to think. "Oh," said she at last, "I expect I shall look after people, and help anybody I can." Then, turning the tables: "And what will you be when you grow up?"

Brian had his reply all ready. "Oh," said he, "I shall be a comedian. I'd like to make people laugh."

It would never do, of course, for us all to become professional comedians—but I think there is room in this world for any number of folk who are ready to make other people happy.

FRIDAY—AUGUST 19.

MR JOHN did not feel too good—a touch of tummy trouble, no doubt; and the postie had brought no letter from his daughter.

In a word, Mr John was just a little depressed.

So what did he do?

Mr John solved his little problem in his own way. Though by no means well off, he managed to find a pound or so, and away he trotted to the shops, spent over an hour buying oddments such as tinned meat and tinned fruit, a cake or two, some sweets and a bunch of flowers. Then he visited two lone elderly friends, gave each a share of his goods, stayed half an hour telling and hearing the news, and in the evening went to see a friend in hospital, taking him the flowers.

"Funny thing," Mr John told me, "I began the day feeling miserable and ended it feeling fine!"

SATURDAY—AUGUST 20.

ONE night recently the wind howled over my roof, and instantly memory winged me back across the years and miles to that time, when I was only six, aboard a passenger vessel in the notoriously-rough Bay of Biscay.

I was playing deck quoits. Suddenly our ship's siren hooted frantically. With others I hurried to the bulwarks, and saw a large cargo vessel uncomfortably close. I felt our ship swerve as she steered a new course—and the cargo ship was soon astern, tossed by every windswept wave.

Later I was told that, in the storm of the day before, she had lost her rudder and a propeller . . . and was drifting helplessly in a world of waters.

Moving around, but getting nowhere. What a dangerous, futile way of living! Happy the young man or woman who has idealism and determination to move in a straight line towards some chosen end . . . and a sorry spectacle, indeed is he who is merely drifting through life, a danger to others and himself.

SUNDAY—AUGUST 21.

GIVE thanks unto the Lord.

MONDAY—AUGUST 22.

YOU will find this short epitaph on a gravestone in the churchyard in the little town of Rudston, in Yorkshire.

"God give me work
Till my life shall end.
And life, till my work is done."

We could all do worse than remember these words in our prayers.

TUESDAY—AUGUST 23.

THE Rev. Dr Nelson Gray, of Parkhead Congregational Church, spotted four wee boys outside the kirk, with dirty faces, tousled hair, and tattered jerseys. After a whispered consultation, one of them cried—" Mister, can we see inside your church?" Of course, Dr Gray didn't refuse—and off they went together.

The laddies stared in wide-eyed wonder at the Communion table, the gold and red carpet in the chancel, the stained-glass window with its portrait of the Good Shepherd with a little lamb in his arms. " It's great..." breathed the littlest one in a reverential whisper.

But the climax came with their visit to the pulpit. They peered over the edge, and gazed in awe over the rows of empty seats and silent galleries.

Then one of them noticed the glass and jug of water on the pulpit shelf. " What's that for?" he inquired. Before Dr Gray could reply, one of the others stepped in. " That's what he does the babies with," he declared. The oldest laddie glared at them both with scorn. " Ach, don't be so daft," he snorted. " That's what he drinks when he talks too much!"

So the visit ended—but Dr Gray won't forget his wee, dirty-faced deputation for a long time.

WEDNESDAY—AUGUST 24.

SUCH lots of lovely things there are
    In this old world of ours—
The sunshine, mountains, lakes and streams,
    And birds and trees and flowers.
Grant, Lord, that I may find each day
    Of loveliness a store,
A wealth of bright and happy things
    Which I may thank Thee for.

THE FRIENDSHIP BOOK

As a 15-year-old, he was expelled from school because, said the headmaster, his lack of interest in his studies was a bad influence on his classmates.

So he sat an examination to gain entry to a different school—and failed to pass it.

At length he found a place in yet another school, finished his training and applied for a post as a teacher. He was turned down.

Then he got a job as a tutor in a boarding school —and was promptly dismissed. Finally, and only by the influence of his family, he managed to get a humble job in an office.

Layabout. Dunce. Failure. In his time, he was known as all of these. Yet he went on to become a university professor, a Nobel prize-winner, and one of the greatest teachers, mathematicians and physicists the world has ever known.

His name was Albert Einstein.

I was pleased to catch sight of my friend George the other morning—he on one side of the road, I on the other. We were lads at school together, so we know each other very well. I raised a hand. George did the same.

And what a lot better he looked—not stooping quite so much; a bit of colour in his cheeks. And he was walking along the pavement more quickly than I have seen for years.

So I crossed the street to tell George he looked years younger. . .

But I never mentioned that.

It wasn't George. It was George's youngest son. Now and then I suspect that I am as old as I am.

SATURDAY—AUGUST 27.

BIG BEN chiming the hour has echoed through our homes for many years.

I wonder if you know the old verse that can be sung to the Westminster chimes?

" All through this hour, God be my guide;
And by Thy power, no ill betide."

SUNDAY—AUGUST 28.

BLESSED are the peacemakers: for they shall be called the children of God.

MONDAY—AUGUST 29.

IN church one Sunday we sang the hymn " God Who Made The Earth." I can never sing it without picturing the countryside in summer time, and thinking of sunshine and blue skies. As it was played over on the organ, I found myself wondering about the woman who wrote it.

She was Sarah Bradshaw, a humble working girl, who was born in Sheffield more than 130 years ago. She was a simple, honest soul with a simple, sunny faith that carried her and her family through many dark days.

Then she married and became Sarah Rhodes— and one day she was asked if she would write a new hymn for a special service for little children. The hymn she wrote was the lovely hymn we sang that Sunday:—

God, who made the earth,
The air, the sky, the sea,
Who gave the light its birth,
Careth for me.

In the six simple verses of Sarah Rhodes' hymn you will find a firm foundation for a lasting faith.

TUESDAY—AUGUST 30.

THE Lady of the House and I were talking about posties we have known, unhonoured and unsung, but all of them trudging in summer heat without complaining, bending to the winter with splendid stubbornness—and doing their job in city or widespread rural areas as if aware that much depended on it.

"There was jovial Jack who drove the parcels' van," the Lady of the House reminded me. "You ran off with more than one of his stories!"

"And Stephen the soldier," said I. "You sent his wife a few dainties when she was ill, and do you remember how he came and cleaned the windows when we couldn't get anybody else?"

"And Peter. Always whistling, always cheery—and always on the lookout for stamps for that boy of his. It nearly broke his heart when he died so young."

"But he kept on whistling!"

"So he did. And somehow that reminds me of Little John, as we used to call him years ago. You remember? He died suddenly—and how proud, how very proud he would have been if he'd lived to see both his sons work their way to university!"

So we went on . . . Not all posties are saints and angels, but most of them are grand folk; and in all weathers I raise my hat to them . . . the posties deserve a pat on the back, surely?

WEDNESDAY—AUGUST 31.

I NEVER forget those words of Charles Reade :—
"*Not a day passes but men and women of no note do great deeds, speak great words, and suffer noble sorrows.*"

SEPTEMBER

I CAME across-this quotation from Dr J. Richard Sneed, of Los Angeles. Speaking about Americans, he said:—

There are six things we can never afford as a nation—intolerance, indolence, injustice, indifference, intemperance, and ingratitude.

Wherever any of these enter they lead to deterioration, defeat, and disaster. Any nation given to them inevitably falls.

What is true of Americans is true of us all.

I HEARD the other day of a medical student at university who found life tough going.

With a big examination ahead, the student felt as if he had never five minutes to spare, and was all the time terribly conscious that those at home who had sacrificed a good deal for his sake would be disappointed if he failed.

There came a day when he felt he must certainly lose the battle—the revision he had to do seemed to him to be more than he could cope with—and there were so many other demands upon him. Young men don't easily lose heart, but tired as he was and with his nerves jangling, this medical student was heading for disaster.

Who was it, I wonder, who sensed all this? Neither the student himself nor I has a clue to the answer.

But one morning the student found under his door a note which read:— When there is no peril in the fight there is no glory in the triumph.

That set the student firmly on his feet!

SATURDAY—SEPTEMBER 3.

"I'VE been busy collecting for a good cause," said a friend. "Folk have been polite, on the whole, and few have shut the door in my face, but a shilling has been quite a large gift, and the number of half-crowns hasn't been anything marvellous.

"But one afternoon I called at a door and knocked. I heard a voice inviting me to walk in. I found a little old lady who could manage to hobble across the floor with two sticks, but preferred sitting by the fire. And how she chattered, and what questions she asked ! I was there half an hour, and it went in a flash.

"And she gave me five shillings ! When I protested that it was too much she laughed like a schoolgirl and said, 'All my life I've given till it hurt.' "

I'm wondering if the happiest people of all are those who not only give—money, time, thought, service—but give till it hurts.

SUNDAY—SEPTEMBER 4.

PERSECUTED, but not forsaken ; cast down, but not destroyed.

MONDAY—SEPTEMBER 5.

MAY I pass on five little words ?

You may think that so few words can mean nothing and be of no value, but they were written by a very great thinker of the 18th century, and they are a challenge to all that is best in you, an assurance that life can be lived finely, and an inspiration if, by any chance, you are undecided.

And here, without more ado, are these five little words—" I ought, therefore I can."

THE FRIENDSHIP BOOK

RAISE a cheer for two lads from Edinburgh who enjoyed a week's holiday in Scarborough!

They were staying with an aunt who has a first-floor flat overlooking a very busy road near the sea —a road which, at this time of the year, is busiest of all at the week-end.

In the basement flat lives a widower of 80 and his daughter. The old man, partly paralysed, weighs over fifteen stones. Much of his time he is in bed, and when he does get up for an hour or two, all he can do is sit in a chair, well propped up with cushions.

And he has lived a very active, busy life . . . and he loves crowds!

Hearing of this, the two lads fixed things. They got the old man into his armchair. They trussed him up like a fowl. Then, one lad in front and the other behind, they heaved him slowly up a narrow and crooked stair, and left him in the window of the first-floor flat.

For half a Sunday that lonely invalid looked down on the surging crowds, saw the cars and the colour, heard the noise, felt again the thrill of being among folk. It was the biggest thrill he had had for a long time . . . and it rather thrilled the lads also!

FULL many a race is lost
  Ere ever a step is run,
And many a coward fails
  Ere ever his work's begun.
Think big—and your deeds will grow.
  Think small, and you'll fall behind.
Think that you can—and you will . . .
  It's all in the state of your mind!

THE FRIENDSHIP BOOK

A YOUNG man and woman stood in the vestry of East and Belmont Church, Aberdeen.

They told the minister that they were newly-married and had come to make their home in Aberdeen. For the past month or two they had enjoyed visiting churches in the city, but it wasn't until they went to East and Belmont that they decided this was the church for them. " You see," they said to the minister, " we've found it such a friendly church."

Now, the remarkable thing is that this young man and his wife are both blind. They could not see the beauty of the church they had come to; they could not know if the congregation looked glad to see them, and they didn't see the warm smiles of welcome that met them at the door.

But, blind as they are, they felt the atmosphere of friendliness all around them, and they did not need their eyes to tell them they were indeed among friends.

The question that remains, of course, is how that young couple would have felt if they'd walked into your church—or mine?

HAVE you heard about the twins who were visited by the doctor while recovering from measles? Obviously one greatly admired the medical man—or perhaps longed to use a stethoscope. Anyhow, she declared—" When I grow up I'm going to be a doctor !"

The other twin somehow regarded this as criticism of her mother, for she immediately sat up in bed and said dramatically—" I'm not ! I'm going to be a simple woman just like Mummy !"

SATURDAY—SEPTEMBER 10.

I TICKED him off good and proper. I told him to his face just what I thought of him, which wasn't much. I said he had been irritable without excuse, and that there was just no need to be always in a rush. I informed him that he owed his wife a little more of his time and attention, and that he ought to pull up his socks and plan some happy surprise for her.

Oh, yes, I told him straight.

And he didn't answer back.

The two of us were in the bathroom the other morning, and I think my plain speaking did the man in the mirror quite a bit of good.

SUNDAY—SEPTEMBER 11.

WHEN a man's ways please the Lord, he maketh even his enemies to be at peace with him.

MONDAY—SEPTEMBER 12.

ONE day I met a business man, shrewd and successful, who told me quite frankly that he has an unusual hobby. Every Sunday evening he chooses a Bible text, and makes a point of meditating on it whenever he has a chance each weekday. In bus or train, when walking home, he turns that text over, thinks about it, dwells on it—or, as he put it, with a smile—runs away with it in his mind. He says it is a wonderfully enriching pastime.

When I asked if he was always able to make one text last a whole week, he replied, smiling again, " I've managed every week for over ten years— every week except one, and that was when I meditated three weeks on the words:— God so loved the world."

THE FRIENDSHIP BOOK

WE drove to the hills and worshipped with the congregation in a little country church. Then we found a pleasant spot in the autumn sunshine for our picnic lunch. On every side were fields, swollen with the goodness of the earth and bursting with golden ripeness.

It made me think of the great harvest hymn, " Come, ye thankful people, come," and I couldn't help feeling it must have been on such a day that Henry Alford was inspired to write it.

Alford was vicar of the village of Wymeswold, in Leicestershire, and his congregation were country folk. If any man was an example to his flock, he was, for to him every blade of grass was a miracle of creation, and his heart overflowed at the boundless grace of God.

Something of this has come down to us in his harvest hymn, and I believe that everyone who can should look over the fields at harvest time, as we did. For it gives fresh meaning to Henry Alford's timeless words which we sing at our harvest thanksgiving—

> *Lord of Harvest, grant that we*
> *Wholesome grain and pure may be . . .*

> *SMILE a bit, joke a bit,*
> *Help push life along;*
> *If you're feeling very blue,*
> *Sing a little song.*
>
> *Once the habit comes to stay,*
> *You will find that you*
> *Are not just cheering up yourself,*
> *You're helping others too!*

THE FRIENDSHIP BOOK

As I went into the office I said, "Nice to see you, John. I've a wee story for you—it won't take a minute."

"Bet you a halfpenny it takes five," said John.

And he won his little bet—for it took me six minutes to relate what had happened—much to my amazement.

It made me think. It made me think a lot. It made me realise that most of us talk too much and use too many words, and that all of us waste a lot of time talking. Now indeed I understand just what the minister meant when he declared, "If you like I will try to preach for less time than usual, but my sermon is such that it will take a long time to make it shorter."

According to a very old story, there was once a Roman teenager who, after some practice with a weapon, complained that his sword was too short.

"In that case," said his father, "you must add a step to it."

I like that. It may be that in the battle of life you lack skill or money or influence, and imagine that because your sword is too short you cannot win a victory. But if you add a step to it—go forward bravely, get nearer to the problem, fight harder, or wait more patiently, give your heart and mind and strength to the immediate task or problem, the chances are that, ill-equipped though you may seem, you will win through.

It is not so much the length of your sword that counts—it is the determination of the fighter.

THE FRIENDSHIP BOOK

TAKE care of your temper. Don't let it slip. Hold on to it whatever you do. It can cause endless suffering and ruin the home, break up the family, turn heaven to hell, hurt more than a burn or scald, and make you terribly poor because nobody loves you.

And one other thing. As the Chinese say—" If you lose your temper it is a sure sign that you are in the wrong."

BETTER is a dinner of herbs where love is, than a stalled ox and hatred therewith.

" THERE goes a nitwit," remarked my friend Andrew, as a young man overtook us on the pavement.

I glanced at Andrew. He is big and broad and genial, and remarks of that kind are not usual. " Meaning ?" I inquired.

" Why," boomed Andrew, " I met him yesterday when he was in no end of a bad temper. He and his wife—they haven't been married two years yet—had had a tiff, it seems, and he told me he was determined to make it plain who was boss in his house !"

" Well ?" I asked, not seeing daylight.

" Well," rumbled Andrew, grinning, " I gave him a bit of good advice, but he won't take it. I told him I'd been married nearly forty years, and that a married man was a great deal happier if he never found out who was boss."

And I rather think Andrew is right.

THE FRIENDSHIP BOOK

A LITTLE over six years ago I received a heart-breaking letter from the mother of a girl of sixteen.

She told me her daughter had undergone an operation, that she was making no headway, and that it was only a matter of time . . . she was dying.

I replied in the only way I knew, assuring her that she and her daughter were in our thoughts and prayers, and that my wife and I were sharing this agony of her mind and heart.

Recently I have received from the same address a piece of wedding cake, and my wife and I have shared it and have enjoyed it all the more because the girl who was dying did not die and is now happily married.

An odd thought strikes me. Because the Lady of the House and I shared in the anxiety six years ago we are now sharing in the happiness of today. Somehow that seems the pattern of living . . . not to stand aside, not to be too engrossed in one's own affairs; not to dodge the shadows and search only for sunshine . . . but to take joys and sorrows, good times and bad, as they come. That is living.

G OLDEN tints of autumn
    Shining in the trees,
Golden sun at evening,
    Rustling of the breeze;
Happy hours spent walking
    Through the falling leaves;
Then home to warmth and friendship—
    Nothing more could please!

" IN MEMORIAM "

To think that on this very spot eternities ago
    Some simple folk like you and me were gently laid in earth !
Will someone come to visit us in a thousand years or so,
    And, like us, ponder mysteries of life and death and birth ?

DAVID HOPE

FAITH

When nature's red in tooth and claw
It's instinct makes us tough.
But faith from deeper springs can draw
When instinct's not enough.

DAVID HOPE

THURSDAY—SEPTEMBER 22.

A FRIEND wrote to say that he had spent two nights in a very expensive, frightfully modern London hotel where there were a great many guests, all of them well-to-do, otherwise they could not have afforded to buy a sandwich there !

" The second evening I was there, Francis," he wrote, " I left the lounge and took a stroll round the block. The sun had set, but the sky was red. I strolled out of the palatial foyer into the street, and a minute or two later walked under the kitchen windows of the hotel. They were wide open, and near one of them was a large Negress polishing wine glasses—and singing with all her heart and soul, her face lit up with happiness.

" An odd thought struck me. I had been in that expensive hotel 48 hours—and the only person who looked radiantly happy was a washer-up in the hot kitchen. It made me think."

As for me, I am still thinking about it !

FRIDAY—SEPTEMBER 23.

WE met at a street corner. " 'Morning, Angus," I sang out. " I've been meaning to drop in and have a word with you."

The middle-aged man, spare and gaunt, assumed a fierce manner. " Oh," he snapped, " the road to hell is paved with good intentions."

He rasped out the words in a way which would have made me tremble but for the twinkle in his eyes. Then he added, " But it has been said that good intentions have their place in heaven, too. So I'll forgive you !"

Then Angus beamed on me.

For all that, as I told myself, intending to do a thing is never quite the same as actually doing it !

THE FRIENDSHIP BOOK

TO those on holiday as to those at home, to those with money to spare and those with scarcely enough to live on, to the young and the old, to the sick and the well, I commend that old Servian proverb—*The best people are the first to thank and the last to complain.*

OF the increase of His government and peace there shall be no end.

I HEARD recently about an Argentine school for boys which overlooks a sharp and dangerous bend in an important road. It seems that, in spite of this kink in the highway being notorious, there are at least two or three lorry drivers a week who fail to slow down sufficiently, with the result that the vehicle slides into the grassy bank on the right and turns over.

Whenever this happens a team of quite small boys set the lorry back on the road in next to no time—and enjoy doing it.

Indeed, the school keeps a long rope expressly for this one job.

No sooner is a lorry ditched than out troop the schoolboys, the rope is attached, and the boys pull together, steadily, expertly, and with confidence—and the lorry is righted.

One of those laddies could not do it. Neither could two or three—but a team can do it, and do it easily—*as long as there are no slackers and as long as everybody pulls his weight !*

Here endeth the sermon.

THE FRIENDSHIP BOOK

THEY came from North and South, and both arrived by the same post.

The first letter I opened was from a " young " man of 84 and tells me that he has bought some books, and begun studying French. " It's quite an adventure," declares this student, " and you don't know what a lot of fun I've got out of it. I find I can translate French into English more easily than I can turn English into French—but I must press on, may be in a year or two . . ."

And the second letter I opened was from a charming " young" lady of 79 who tells me in confidence that she has been very busy—on and off —for the last twelve months. Whenever she has a spare half-hour she writes her life story. She adds—

" It's simply thrilling, Francis, to sit a wee while and think myself back to some particular period of my life, and then try to recall the details—where I was and who I met and what they said. And then putting it all down on paper, and seeing it grow, and feeling that perhaps my children may read it when I'm gone . . . I've been better in health since I took up this hobby."

Well, doesn't it all go to show that it's never too late to begin ?

NOW summer with its friendly days is slipping swiftly by,
Now early sets the glowing sun and birds now southward fly;
Good-bye to long, bright, sunny days—but why should I complain ?
There never was a winter yet but summer came again !

THE FRIENDSHIP BOOK

I OPENED the book to look for one thing, and while hunting I found another—a short sentence which made me think. I read—It is wicked to grow accustomed to things which are good.

Forgetting what I was actually in search of, I thought hard about this sentence, written by Publius Surius over 2000 years ago, not sure at first just what it meant.

I think I understand. Do not we say in these days that familiarity breeds contempt? And is it not true that many of us grow quite used to the good things of this life—freedom, health and strength, labour-saving gadgets, pleasures, and so on—and therefore fail to value them as we should or realise, as we ought, how fortunate we are? Millions of people have none of these things. It makes you think.

And it should make us thankful!

THE Lady of the House walked a little way with Mrs Gray. "You have a heavy bag," my wife remarked.

"Yes," Mrs Gray agreed, smiling, "it's pretty heavy, but I like doing it. Most mornings, if fine, I go along to the shops, do my own bit of shopping, and buy in this and that for Mrs Davidson. She's fond of sweet things, and likes them fresh, and I sometimes take her a tin of something extra or a pot of something she hasn't asked for."

Then, with an arch smile—"You know, my dear, when a body gets to be eighty-three it's all you can do to help her a wee bit!"

The Lady of the House assures me that she kept a straight face as she said seriously, "Why, of course!"

Mrs Gray, I might mention, is well over 75!

OCTOBER

TAKE care when throwing stones. Watch out when trying to put other people in their proper place.

And keep in mind this little story of one customer to another in a grocer's shop—"How did that naughty little boy of yours get hurt yesterday?"

The other customer smiled graciously—indeed, charmingly—as she replied—"That good little boy of yours hit him on the head with a stick."

SET your heart and your soul to seek the Lord your God.

WILLIE is a coalman. He is a quiet man, with a ready smile and strong hands.

But Willie doesn't just deliver the coal—where old folk are concerned, he does very much more. For instance, if old Mrs B—— hasn't got her fire going, Willie gets down on his knees, sweeps out the grate, sets it with paper, sticks and coal, and, before he leaves, he sees there's a cheery blaze going.

Or if there are some extra big lumps of coal in the bag he's taken to an old lady, he cheerfully breaks them up for her—and, like as not, carries out the ashes, too.

There are many old people whom Willie helps week by week. I know Willie would be the last man to lay claim to a halo for all this, but, by jove, if each of us put that wee bit extra into his job, as Willie does, what a difference it would make.

TUESDAY—OCTOBER 4.

DURING the war between China and Japan which broke out about 1931, a little Japanese girl who had heard about Christianity was in a desperate plight. The Chinese and the Japanese in that region were fighting. The river broke its banks after heavy rains, and floods cut off some refugees from the approaching Chinese guerillas. The enemy behind and the swirling floods before meant death. The Japanese girl had seen her mother die of starvation. She had seen her father killed. She watched while folk she knew were drowned before her eyes.

But she had faith. Only a little faith, perhaps, mixed with much ignorance. All hope was lost. Death was certain—but the wee maid put her hands together, and prayed—" Please, God, if you love me, save me."

Then she plunged into the water, went under, came up, grasped a horse by its tail, and thus—though she could not swim and was faint from hunger—she reached the further side, and was safe.

It all sounds incredible yet it happened, and that little maid is now happily married, and she and her husband are preaching the Christian faith in a far land.

WEDNESDAY—OCTOBER 5.

A LITTLE house where one may sing,
A little work to do;
A little child to love and train—
Of blessings just a few.
A man who has a little smile,
A little hug or kiss . . .
Oh, let the great recline in state,
A little wealth means bliss!

THE FRIENDSHIP BOOK

SIR WINSTON CHURCHILL was afraid of nothing—not even of death. Indeed, he spoke many times of his passing, and always he looked upon it as a man of faith, confident that, when it came, he would go forward into the unknown without fear.

Once he said—" The older you get, the more sleep you need. Finally, you sleep all the time. In life there are many avenues, but all lead in the end to kindly, all-embracing death."

These, surely, were the words of a man not afraid to meet his Maker. And what more fitting farewell could he have bidden us than these words of his own, spoken many years ago, but so poignantly appropriate today—

" Good night, then. Sleep to gather strength for the morning, for the morning will come. Brightly will it shine on the brave and true, kindly upon all who suffer for the cause, glorious upon the tombs of heroes. Thus will shine the dawn..."

" ANOTHER dull morning," grumbled the guest to the hotel porter who was cleaning the brass handle of the front door. " If you ask me, it'll be raining before we've finished breakfast."

" And so it might, sir," agreed the porter, polishing away till the handle shone. " There's no telling. We could have a downpour that lasts all day for anything you and I know, sir. But, looking back over the years, sir, I've known a lot of dull mornings become sunny afternoons."

" H'm !" snorted the guest, and turned on his heel.

And the hotel porter kept on polishing.

SATURDAY—OCTOBER 8.

I LIKE the story of the English tourist and the old Highland shepherd.

The tourist was recuperating after a nervous breakdown and was trying desperately to find not only health and strength, but also courage to battle on.

It was then he fell in with the old shepherd. They walked and talked together; and the tourist, looking up at the mountains from the track in the valley, remarked: " I suppose there's no way over those heights ?"

" Oh, but there is," replied the shepherd. " You can't see it from the valley, but if you follow the winding track, and keep plodding on and up you'll cross the ridge, and reach the further side."

That was the message the Englishman needed— that was the source of the courage he found, the inspiration which gave him a new lease of life.

SUNDAY—OCTOBER 9.

HAVE mercy upon me, O God, according to Thy loving kindness.

MONDAY—OCTOBER 10.

HAVE you heard about the boy who was seen hanging on grimly to the lead of a very big dog ? When somebody asked where he was taking the dog, he replied—" I'm not taking him anywhere. I'm just finding out where he wants to go."

I cannot help thinking that is a kind of parable. So many people who scorn religion make a poor thing of life by going the way they want to go rather than finding out which way God would have them go—and then, in His strength, going that way.

TUESDAY—OCTOBER 11.

HE was one of four decorators who swooped down upon us, and began painting the exterior of the house. They were four cheery workmen doing the job in first-class style ... all except one who was apt to be rather careless.

Poor fellow, it was not a criminal offence. I expect he was not giving his mind to the job. All I know is that he gave the front gate a coat of priming without first removing the little metal nameplate. Two screws to unscrew—only that.

" Why," exclaimed the Lady of the House, " you haven't removed the plate ! I don't like decorators to paint round it—the job never looks professional, and it's just not the way to do it !" She paused, looking at the offending nameplate. Then—" Drop your brush ! Let's have the nameplate off here and now !"

So off it came !

Not a bit like the Lady of the House, really ... but, as she says, if there's a right way to do a job, it should be done that way !

And I must not forget to add that having forgiven the erring decorator, the Lady of the House handed him a cup of tea and a generous slice of cake ... with a smile !

WEDNESDAY—OCTOBER 12.

GARDENS are such pleasant things,
Away from shop or street.
There you may chat with friendly folk
Who grow nice things to eat ...
Or watch the golden sun go down,
Or stand awhile or sit,
Or think in peace or dream and dream,
Or even dig a bit.

THE FRIENDSHIP BOOK

HOW do you assess the value of anything?

I am thinking of a little picture about seven inches by four. It is a water colour painting of a Scottish glen. I should think the paper is worth a few pence, and the home-made frame perhaps a shilling or so. Would half-a-crown be a fair price or possibly three and sixpence?

There it hangs on the wall—near to the fireplace in Mrs MacLeod's living-room; and she told me recently that it is worth just about everything to her.

The picture was painted by her husband's best friend, John Dun. It depicts part of a glen where Mr and Mrs MacLeod spent many a happy hour. When the painting was finished he framed it, intending to give it to Mr MacLeod as a birthday present. But Mr MacLeod died the day before his birthday, and the artist died the day after Mr MacLeod's funeral.

Mr Dun's widow gave the picture to Mrs MacLeod—and she treasures it above rubies.

Do you wonder?

ON my way home one evening I overtook three unkempt youths who were sauntering along, jostling each other, getting nowhere, laughing harshly, and I suppose it was by contrast that there came to me words spoken of David Livingstone:—

I remember his step after forty years, a characteristic forward tread, firm, simple, resolute, neither fast nor slow but which evidently meant getting there.

And how I wished those three thoughtless, time-wasting youths had had an end in view, and were striding towards it.

SATURDAY—OCTOBER 15.

I HAD to go to the function.

Frankly, I abominate evening dinners and dress suits and a lot of starch and talk and hand-clapping—but there was no way out, so I went. And the Lady of the House eyed me carefully, adjusted my bow, found a speck of dust on my impeccable black, asked if I had a spare hanky, told me to be careful coming out of a hot room into the cold night air . . .

And I gave her a kiss and hurried off—hurried because I was anxious to be back, thinking all the time that a truly loving wife will do anything, anything for her husband except stop trying to improve him !

SUNDAY—OCTOBER 16.

THE Lord is good ; His mercy is everlasting ; and His truth endureth to all generations.

MONDAY—OCTOBER 17.

" I LIKE wash days," she said to the Lady of the House.

She is a wife and the mother of two young children, and she has an invalid mother living with her.

But what a bright, lovable, cheery, busy, sensible, and imaginative person she is.

" Like wash days ?" my wife repeated.

" Yes," was the reply. " I don't like thinking on Friday of Monday's wash—and it's an effort to dismiss it on Saturday and Sunday. But when Monday comes, heigh-ho, I battle along, glad to be doing it, delighted to get to the ironing—and, oh, my, how wonderful to wake on Tuesday morning and know I haven't to wash for a week !"

THE FRIENDSHIP BOOK

I HAVE mentioned my great aunt, Maggie, more than once. She was the warmest-hearted and the most generous-minded of women—and the only time I ever remember her being harsh or contemptuous was when somebody referred to a neighbour's sewing.

"Sewing!" snapped my great aunt. "All the sewing that body can do is unravelling!"

The verdict has lived with me all down the years. For anything I know, it was unjust, but I doubt it. I rather think my great aunt was ready to forgive anything except pulling to pieces.

After all, there is something to be said for doing a bit of sewing, even if it is badly done. But unravelling a bit of knitting . . . well, anybody can do it, and nothing much is achieved when it is done.

Debunking great folk is like knocking down pins in a mini bowl . . . and people who are most ready and willing to unravel the lives of good folk should take care, for after all they are exposing their own unpleasant nature and their own pitiful littleness of spirit since only those with a bit of greatness in them can really value greatness when they see it in others.

AT seventeen our Annie's not a stained-glass window saint—
Those roguish, twinkling eyes of hers, that laugh without restraint!

Yet, homeward running from her job she'll turn aside, will Annie,
To buy some tasty little treat . . . her gift, with love, to Granny!

I WISH him luck.

I'm thinking of Alec. He is 31. He has a really charming wife and a son and heir who has just cut his first tooth. He has a delightful little home— and there is not a penny owing on it, or on anything in it. He was poor enough when he started up in business on his own, but now he is doing amazingly well, and friends and neighbours say he has been lucky.

That is just where I disagree with Alec's friends and neighbours. It seems to me there has been precious little luck, if any.

For the truth is, that while some of Alec's contemporaries have been waiting for the luck of the draw or hoping something will turn up, Alec has been working, working hard, working long hours—and using his wits.

So, when I say I wish him luck, I mean that I hope he will have health and strength to go on doing well—he deserves to.

THERE is just no understanding women.

For instance, the other morning I found the Lady of the House cleaning her oldest pair of shoes —a pair of wrinkled brogues. She had been using them for a spot of gardening, and she was busy scraping off chunks of hard soil.

" What's the big idea ?" I asked.

" Cleaning shoes," said she.

" But why ? If ever you wear them again you'll wear them for gardening or going up a muddy lane on a wet day."

The Lady of the House looked at me rather pityingly as she replied—" However muddy they get next time, I'll want them clean to begin with !"

SATURDAY—OCTOBER 22.

WITHIN two minutes' walk of the Bank of England—in the very heart of London—is an expensively furnished office, an office where important decisions are made, an office belonging to an expert who is certainly a very successful somebody in the city.

It is, therefore, significant that on the polished desk is a very small white card in a frame. It reads:— For one man that can stand prosperity, a hundred will stand adversity.

SUNDAY—OCTOBER 23.

STRAIT is the gate, and narrow is the way, which leadeth unto life.

MONDAY—OCTOBER 24.

MRS GORDON was being driven through Dublin in a taxi.

As the taxi reached a busy crossing the driver slammed on his brakes. All around, cars, buses, lorries, and vans, came to a sudden stop. A boy, waving his arms, dashed from the pavement out into the traffic, bringing it to a standstill.

Yet the amazing thing was that not a horn was sounded. Not an angry word was heard. Why? Because in the middle of the road lay a pigeon which had been injured by a passing car—and the sharp-eyed laddie had spotted it and stopped the traffic to save it.

Patiently, the drivers waited, smiling, as the boy picked up the bird and carried it to the pavement. Then, slowly, the traffic began to move again, and soon all was back to normal. " And," added Mrs Gordon, " we got there just the same."

THE FRIENDSHIP BOOK

WHENEVER you are tempted to say an unkind word or take a mean advantage of anybody or hurt somebody by poking fun at them, or by slick action gain an advantage, say " Shu."

I dare say this sounds nonsense, but it is not as absurd as it may appear.

Everybody, of course, is familiar with Christ's golden rule—Whatsoever ye would that men should do unto you, do ye even so to them, for this is the law and the prophets. In a word—Do as you would be done by.

This is the way to live, and we know it, but not all of us are aware that Confucius, the great Chinese sage, said very much the same thing nearly 500 years before Christ.

The teaching of Confucius may be summed up in the sentence—" What you do not like done to you do not to others." This is rather clumsy, but it can be shortened to " Reciprocity." And the whole meaning and teaching and challenge of the idea can be expressed by a single Chinese character—the character " Shu."

How are you to live finely ? By shaping your life according to " Shu."

SO many things there are each day
To make us sad or mad;
So often we must sigh because
We've lost some joys we had.

So much might have been otherwise —
We've troubles by the score;
And yet how true of me (and YOU) —
We've much to thank God for !

THURSDAY—OCTOBER 27.

MANY years ago a New York housewife sat down in the quietness of her home and drew pen and paper towards her.

When she rose she had written one of the best hymns of all —" I need Thee every hour."

Her name was Annie Sherwood Hawks. She died 46 years ago, and the remarkable thing is that, apart from what I have told you, almost nothing is known of her. Yet, perhaps that is the very reason why her hymn has become so beloved, for it speaks in simple words of the faith of a humble soul.

I need Thee every hour, in joy or pain
Come quickly and abide, or life is vain . . .

To me, the wonderful thing about the hymn is that, in four simple verses, it says everything that a prayer should say.

I need Thee every hour, Teach me Thy will,
And Thy rich promises in me fulfil . . .

FRIDAY—OCTOBER 28.

TO take up a new hobby when you are turned 70 is, surely, no easy task, but that is precisely what Mr Matson has done. All his life he has been a keen gardener, but an illness has put a stop to digging and pruning and potting.

So Mr Matson has bought himself a box of paints, a brush, and some paper. He has collected quite a few wise or witty sayings, and has set to work to print the words with a pen and illuminate them with many-coloured flowers, all to make a most attractive little gift for friends and neighbours to hang in their homes.

" It takes a bit of doing when you're a complete novice," Mr Matson assured me. " But that's why I like it—if it were easy I wouldn't bother."

THE FRIENDSHIP BOOK

MY watch was going slow, so I took it to a watch-maker. He asked me when I wound it. I said I wound it last thing every night.

" Always wind your watch first thing in the morning," he said. " If you do that, sir, I don't think you'll have any more trouble."

During the day a watch must cope with many jars and jerks. If the watch has been wound the night before, the tension of the spring is weaker, and it can't withstand shocks so well. But a watch that's wound in the morning can take all these in its stride. " So, you see, sir," he concluded, " it's always better to begin the day with a strong spring."

Well, I took his advice—and my watch now keeps perfect time. I'm grateful to the jeweller for that, but I'm also grateful to him for giving me this splendid parable—for if we, too, begin the day with a strong spring, be it from a prayer or a quiet moment with the Good Book, how can we fail to make the very best of it ?

SIRS, ye are brethren; why do ye wrong one to another?

A HOUSEWIFE recently moved into a new house. She tells me that her small kitchen is a delight, and that in it she keeps these lines written for her by a friend in Ireland:—

Bless my little kitchen, Lord.
I love its every look.
And guide me as I do my best,
Especially when I cook !

NOVEMBER

TUESDAY—NOVEMBER 1.

OUTSIDE the sky was black, a freezing sleet was driving through the town, and the streets were deep in chill, grey slush.

Even the warm lights of the church couldn't disguise the kind of night it was; the few who had braved the weather waited, damp and perhaps a little depressed, for the service to begin.

Then, with a smile, the minister announced the first hymn—and you'd never guess in a hundred years what it was. Why, it was the cheeriest and brightest of all hymns, " Summer suns are glowing, over land and sea !" And by the time the congregation sat down they simply couldn't have cared less about the weather !

Isn't it true that, even when it's winter here, summer suns are glowing elsewhere ? What's more, doesn't it mention clouds and dark skies in the third verse ?

So I dare to hope we'll hear the hymn sung in a good many more churches the whole year through —for you can't help feeling that life's a lot sunnier for singing it !

WEDNESDAY—NOVEMBER 2.

WHEN you are feeling down and out
    And just a little blue,
It isn't wise to sit about—
    And moan the whole day through.

Just try to be more cheerful, for
    You'll find it well worth while.
So count your blessings o'er and o'er—
    And try to wear a smile !

THE FRIENDSHIP BOOK

A NEW chapel was dedicated in the tiny village of Garrynamonie, on the southernmost tip of the isle of South Uist, in the Hebrides. When the chapel was being planned, Father McKellaig, the parish priest, wondered how best the great message of faith could be symbolised—and he thought of a splendid idea.

Why not place a cross on the highest wall of the chapel, where it could be lit up at night, and from where it would shine out over the sea ?

It was a fine idea. The cross is five feet high, so that not only the villagers can see it, but fishermen can use it to steer by through the narrow sound between Barra and Uist, and it is a landmark to all other ships that pass by.

May all who see it be guided safely, not only by its light, but also by the message it proclaims.

MRS ROBERTSON is blind—but it would be hard to find anyone more cheerful. Her minister asked her how she managed to keep so cheerful all the time.

Mrs Robertson thought for a moment, then she said—" There are three things that keep me going. First, my old-age pension; second, my faith; and third, my favourite text, which is ' My grace is sufficient for thee.' "

So, with her pension, her faith, and her infinite trust in God's grace, this blind old lady still finds life a joy and a challenge that many, richer by far in this world's goods, would give all they have to possess.

And so real is her faith that it's as much a part of her life as her pension.

SATURDAY—NOVEMBER 5.

I LIKE this old story about John Clerk of Eldin whose son became a famous Scottish lawyer. One of his proudest remarks was, " I remember the time when people, seeing my son, John, limping in the street, asked, ' Whose lame lad is that ? ' And the answer would be, ' He's the son of Clerk of Eldin.' But now, when I myself am passing, I hear them saying, ' What old grey-haired man is that ? ' and the answer is, ' He's the father of John Clerk.' "

SUNDAY—NOVEMBER 6.

HE that is slow to wrath is of great understanding.

MONDAY—NOVEMBER 7.

CHANCE took a friend of mine to a house in a Scottish village—and there he saw something he'd never dreamed of finding. It was an American organ, with an aspidistra on top !

" I came away," said he, " seeing in my mind's eye those Sunday evenings when, after a service in the church, ten or a dozen of us would gather round just such a wheezy instrument. Uncle Robert would suggest a hymn — and away we went, bass and tenor, soprano and contralto."

" It was grand !" he said. " And somehow, next morning, we felt ready for whatever might come."

The world has moved a long way since then. Much has been gained—and something lost. You may smile to think a dozen folk or so could gather round an American organ, crowned with an aspidistra—but only those who have joined in such a little sing-song in the dusk can ever know how much it can mean and what a blessing it can give.

THE FRIENDSHIP BOOK

FOR five years Miss Currie lived in the manse on the little island of North Ronaldsay, in the far north of the Orkneys, and gallantly took the place of a minister to the 140 folk who live there.

When Miss Currie first went to the island, I know her heart was in her mouth, for she could not help wondering how the islanders would accept a woman in the manse. But she needn't have worried. The first thing they asked her to do was to leave the curtains of the manse on the hill undrawn at night, for wherever they were, they wanted to see the light shining from her window.

These five years have been among the happiest she has ever known. In that time she tramped nearly 10,000 miles over the island, visiting crofts and cottages. Sunday by Sunday she led the island folk in prayer, preached the sermon and blessed them with the benediction. As the months passed, every one of the islanders became her close friend.

Now her splendid work is over, for she has retired. But with her she will take memories . . . of evenings round a peat fire in a cottage . . . of family worship in the church . . . and of the joy and sorrow she has been privileged to share.

Who could ask for more?

WE think of those who died so young,
So full of hope, so strong;
With shining dreams of better things,
Their spirits like a song !
And now, when years have brought hot tears
To men grown old and grey,
The gallant dead, untouched by age,
Live in our hearts today.

THE FRIENDSHIP BOOK

IT takes a schoolboy to see things from a different angle.

For instance—

The opposite of evergreen is nevergreen.

Nets are holes surrounded by pieces of string.

Skyscrapers are large telescopes.

A vegetable cell is a place very dark and gloomy where greengrocers who sell bad vegetables go.

Etiquette is the noise you make when you sneeze.

A fort is a place to put men in, a fortress is a place to put women in.

Dust is mud with the juice squeezed out.

ON a cold November morning in France, two men stood together, their faces worn and tired.

The older man was Field Marshal Earl Haig. The other was a young Scots minister who had been his personal chaplain on the battlefields.

It was a moment that neither of them would ever forget—for the armistice that ended the Great War had just been signed.

As well as the triumph and thankfulness that filled Haig's heart, there was another deeper feeling that what he and his men had been through must never happen again.

That is why he turned to his chaplain that day, the ink of his signature on the armistice barely dry, and spoke those words——

" Padre," he said, " you know, your job is to make mine impossible !"

As we remember this morning, let us think also of the words of Earl Haig and strive to work, however humbly, to end the bitterness and strife which blights the memory of those who died.

SATURDAY—NOVEMBER 12.

AT a time when most American artists count themselves lucky if they have a customer now and then, John Edward Harris is selling pictures rapidly and continuously. They're mostly seascapes, done in oils with a knife instead of a brush; and the market for them seems unending.

What's the secret of this young artist's continuing success ? He, himself, told a reporter: " It's the extra five per cent. When I could call a picture finished I don't finish. I go on. I add a bit more of myself. I put in additional touches. I kind of offer a prayer that I shall somehow help somebody to see more beauty. I expect it's a kind of going the second mile."

There seems to me to be a hint for us all in this explanation.

SUNDAY—NOVEMBER 13.

THEY shall beat their swords into plowshares, and their spears into pruninghooks : nation shall not lift up sword against nation, neither shall they learn war any more.

MONDAY—NOVEMBER 14.

THE conversation had turned to the many desperate appeals for help that exist these days—and particularly to the plight of the starving millions in Africa and Asia.

" One can do so very little when you consider the size of the problem," said one of the men. " It makes any effort seem futile."

Then the minister said something I shall remember for a long time. " Don't look on it that way. Remember always—it is better to light a candle than to curse the darkness."

TUESDAY—NOVEMBER 15.

J IM RODGER, a young missionary, died at the hands of the rebels in the Congo.

When the rebel army arrived and announced they were all to be arrested, Jim turned and dashed back into the mission—not in an attempt to escape, but to fill his pockets with little printed texts he used in his work. For he knew what might happen and he realised they might have sore need of God's help and strength when morning came.

That night, as they huddled together in the rebel camp, Jim went round the men and women who lay waiting and wondering, encouraging them with a smile and leaving a text with each of them. The comforting words they read in the text gave them the extra courage they needed—" Thou shalt keep them in perfect peace whose mind is stayed on Thee——"

But Jim did more. For, in the morning, he fearlessly went up to the leader of the rebels and handed a text to him, too, well knowing the risk he took. It was one of the last things he ever did, for a few hours later he was put to death.

The remarkable part of the story is that the rebel leader admitted later to another group of missionaries that he now respected and admired their calling, simply because of the courage of the man who died.

What was the message on the text? I cannot tell you, but how appropriate if it had been, as well it might—" Father, forgive them, for they know not what they do——"

WEDNESDAY—NOVEMBER 16.

I DON'T let the weather bother me a lot—
Storms or deep depressions, cold or very hot.
For I have a secret—weather is my line,
Sunshine? Why, I make it—Life for me is fine!

THE BAY

How is it that a certain place,
A certain view, remains for ever in the heart?
Though we grow old,
Though we may be a thousand miles away,
Still, framed, encompassed, captured in our memory,
Is that first moment when we gazed across the bay.

DAVID HOPE

"AWAY FROM IT ALL"

Let's go for a trek in the sun,
  And feel the cool wind in our face;
Let's ride where the wild rivers run,
  Or rest in some quiet place.

Let's follow the valley down,
    And gaze on that distant peak;
Let's forget that we live in a town—
    Till we go back to work there next week. . . .

DAVID HOPE

THE VOICES FALL SILENT

Song and speech go speeding out
A million minds to link.
How strange to find, where all has birth,
This quiet place to think!

DAVID HOPE

THURSDAY—NOVEMBER 17.

IN my reading the other day I came across a suggestion which was new to me, though perhaps many people are already familiar with it.

The idea was referred to by a Methodist.

He stressed the fact that many folk who regularly attend a place of worship twice on Sunday listen to two sermons, never open their mouths (except to sing), and never really get together apart from a bit of chatter as they come out.

Is there anything to be said in favour of a preaching service on Sunday morning and a less formal gathering on Sunday evening? Would it be a happy thing for church-going men and women of any denomination to discuss the morning sermon at an evening meeting, bringing serious thoughts and a touch of humour to an informal get-together ending with a hymn and a prayer?

I myself do not know the answer. But I think the experiment is well worth talking about.

FRIDAY—NOVEMBER 18.

NOWADAYS, I take a little more care over my handwriting since reading the famous letter which Thomas Bailey Aldrich, the American author, once wrote to a friend—

" It was very pleasant to get your letter the other day. Perhaps I should have found it pleasanter if I had been able to decipher it. I don't think I mastered anything beyond the date (which I knew) and the signature (which I guessed at). There's a singular and perpetual charm in a letter of yours. It never grows old. It never loses its novelty. Other letters are read and thrown away, but yours are kept for ever—unread. One of them will last a reasonable man a lifetime."

SATURDAY—NOVEMBER 19.

THERE'S always a twinkle in old John's eyes.
"—— pity about Mr and Mrs Clark," he was mumbling the other evening. "Can't make a go of it, it seems. Hear there's likely to be a divorce before long. Very sad—and quite unnecessary. The big trouble with some people, you know, is they just won't admit their faults. So silly of them, really."

A long pause. A sudden twinkling of the eyes — "I'd readily admit my faults — if I had any!"

SUNDAY—NOVEMBER 20.

WITH God all things are possible.

MONDAY—NOVEMBER 21.

LEGEND tells of a certain Father Anselm, a monk, who, having wandered into the fields one morning, stood still to listen to a lark. He watched the singing speck soaring into the blue of heaven; and having enjoyed the song, he went back to the monastery for breakfast.

But when he would have entered, a doorkeeper he did not recognise ordered him to wait outside. The doorkeeper asked the monk's name; and when Father Anselm told him, the doorkeeper shook his head, saying no monk of that name belonged to the monastery. Other monks were summoned, all strangers to Father Anselm. At last, having consulted their records, they discovered that a certain Father Anselm had been a member of that fraternity a hundred years before.

Time, it seems, had been blotted out while Father Anselm had been listening to the lark.

And is there any such thing as time when our heart is warmed and our spirit glad?

THE FRIENDSHIP BOOK

PETER was an unwanted child, unloved from the day he was born. As a result, he grew up without trust in people, resentful, afraid.

Of course, he got into trouble. It was only to be expected, for his father and mother neither knew nor cared where Peter went or what he did. At 15 he was sent to a special home, but, despite the patience and friendliness of those who looked after him, they still could not reach through to him.

Then one day he and some of the others were taken to the swimming pool. Suddenly, when no one was watching, a wee girl toddled forward to the water's edge, lost her balance, and fell in.

Before anyone could move, Peter dived into the pool, fully clothed, to save the little girl. When he reached her he took her tenderly in his arms and lifted her out of the water. And when he had scrambled out, he sat down, her arms round his neck, to comfort her.

That was the turning point in Peter's life. Hidden away, deep under the fear and suspicion and distrust, was a boy who wanted to love and be loved, and it had taken the sudden shock of a near-tragedy to bring it to the surface for the first time in his life.

That is not the end of the story, for it will take time to blot out the memories of fifteen years, but it marks a new beginning for Peter.

THE sun may shine and birds may sing,
But little joy you'll find
If you are looking for the worst,
And think all folk unkind.
Though winter's due to stay awhile,
How happy if you've learned to smile!

THURSDAY—NOVEMBER 24.

THE Lady of the House did not go to church on Sunday evening. Both of us are fairly regular attenders—as regular as we can be.

But the Lady of the House was fulfilling a promise. Instead of going to church, she spent an hour or two talking to and keeping an eye on an invalid. This enabled the bedridden lady's daughter to escape from routine, leave the house, attend evening worship, meet a few friends, and thus feel strengthened, cheered, and encouraged for the long days ahead.

Perhaps helping those in need is a form of worship, too ?

FRIDAY—NOVEMBER 25.

IF you have ever passed over the high, lonely road that leads from Moffat to Edinburgh, you will know that for miles there is nothing but wind-swept moorland. But you'll find there one of the nicest gardens you could imagine.

It surrounds an A.A. box by the side of the road, and it is the work of one man—Jack Lees, the patrolman. When he determined to do something to brighten up the road many heads were shaken. How could any flower survive in the biting winds ? How could any seed find life in the stony ground ?

But Jack was undaunted. Passing lorry-drivers dropped bags of rich earth at the box. Jack himself built a little wall to shelter the flowers—and, slowly but surely, the garden took shape.

Now from spring to autumn it's a blaze of colour, everyone who passes is lost in admiration, and many stop to marvel at its beauty.

It would have been easy enough for Jack to leave his little corner of the moor as he found it. But he didn't !

SATURDAY—NOVEMBER 26.

EVERY Sunday morning the service at McCheyne Church, Dundee, is tape-recorded. Then the recording is taken round the old and house-bound.

Now, if you heard one of these tape-recorded services, you would be struck by many features of it —the splendid singing, the prayers, the sermon, and the fine organ music. But you would also hear other things that most of us never notice in church—the coughs and shuffles and creaks and sneezes.

As you'd expect, the old folk are helped by the prayers and sermon, and the hymns and the psalms. But what really intrigues them are these very coughs and shuffles. It makes it all so real, they feel they're actually there.

Which all goes to show that in the eventide the little memories are often the most precious, and the things we take for granted are the finest of all.

SUNDAY—NOVEMBER 27.

THE earth shall be full of the knowledge of the Lord.

MONDAY—NOVEMBER 28.

I RECEIVED a letter from the South of France. I "did" French at school, but that was not the week before last. The Lady of the House knows more of that language than I do, but even her French is a bit rusty. Anyhow, we got the hang of the message—and a very friendly message it was; and there was one sentence both of us could translate more or less straight off.

The sentence, which I now pass on to you for consideration, was — " Un bien fait n'est jamais perdu." And I think a fairly accurate rendering of this might be—" A kindness is never lost."

THE FRIENDSHIP BOOK

A YOUNG man sat in his bedroom, his life in ruins. A few weeks before, his future had seemed bright with promise. He was a joiner, with a good job. He played football and tennis, and he was engaged to marry.

Then came disaster. He lost his sight in a car accident. When he left hospital he had changed from a happy young man into a bitter recluse.

In the midst of his despair the door of his bedroom opened, and a minister walked in. He introduced himself as the Rev. Robin Richmond, and for half an hour, while the young man listened in silence, the minister tried to encourage him.

But it seemed his words fell on stony ground. Why had this happened to him ? the blind man demanded. What good was he to anyone now ? And how could the minister know what he was going through ?

For a moment, Mr Richmond paused. Then, quietly, he said, " But I'm as blind as you are, John !" He went on to explain how he lost his sight during the war, and to tell him of his life since.

It seems the young man's family had seen Mr Richmond on TV and, on impulse, they wrote to him for help. It was the turning point in their son's life. Overnight he became a changed person. He joined his family round the fireside again — he arranged to enter a school for the blind. He has a job.

He knows the way ahead will have its problems — but I'm sure he will succeed.

HOWEVER low you may have sunk,
This splendid truth is plain;
However dead your spirit is,
Life CAN begin again !

DECEMBER

THURSDAY—DECEMBER 1.

BILL SHAPLAND was killed in an accident at sea.

He was serving his apprenticeship in the Merchant Navy, for he had set his heart on the sea, and he was buried at the nearest port, Valetta, in Malta.

It was a grievous blow to his family. But, just when their sorrow was deepest, something happened that, I am sure, made them very proud.

It was simply this. Among those who mourned Bill were his young friends, boys and girls of his own age who could hardly believe they'd never see their chum again. So one evening they met and decided to pay their own tribute to him—a marble stone, paid for from their own pockets, to be laid on his grave.

The memorial was sent from Glasgow to Malta, where the minister who took the burial service placed it on the distant grave. It is just a simple plaque with a short inscription—" In fond remembrance of Bill, from his young friends in Glasgow."

But I know it means more than words can say to those who miss him most.

FRIDAY—DECEMBER 2.

WHEN Johnny came home from a party, his mother, knowing her son's weakness, remarked meaningly : " I hope you didn't ask for a second piece of cake."

Johnny beamed angelically. " I didn't," said he with immense emphasis. " All I did was to ask Mrs Dowson for the recipe so that you could make one like it . . . and she gave me the recipe, and two more pieces of cake, all of her own accord !"

SATURDAY—DECEMBER 3.

I HAPPENED to be speaking to the secretary of the Empire Cancer Campaign.

During our conversation, he took something from his pocket and held it out for me to see. It was a beautiful diamond and sapphire engagement ring, and beside it lay a plain gold wedding ring.

They had been handed to him a few hours earlier by a girl of 21. Only a year before, she and her sweetheart, also in his early twenties, had been married, and no couple could have been happier.

But after a few months, the young man fell suddenly ill with an incurable cancer. Three weeks later he was dead and, at 21, his bride was a heart-broken widow.

What she must have suffered, I cannot even begin to imagine, but I do know she wrote to the secretary asking if he could visit her. When they met, she drew her rings from her finger and handed them to him, asking that they should be used to raise money for the fight against cancer.

Her most precious possessions, once the symbol of her happiness, have, in a way, now become the symbols of hope for others.

SUNDAY—DECEMBER 4.

SING unto the Lord ; for He hath done excellent things.

MONDAY—DECEMBER 5.

THERE are two kinds of really great people in the world—those who can give thoroughly sound advice, and those who can take it. And, of the two, I am not sure but what the latter are greater than the former.

THE FRIENDSHIP BOOK

TIME and again I have seen how tragedy can lead to rich and boundless blessing . . .

One day in 1929 an Edinburgh dentist, Mr John Copland, heard that a close friend's wife had died. She was still a young woman, and Mr Copland knew that if she could have had a blood transfusion, she might not have died.

The more he thought about it, the more he knew something would have to be done—and, single-handed he set about doing it. He enlisted the help of some friends and formed a small group who were willing to give blood for an emergency transfusion.

For years he ran a 24-hour service almost unaided. He slept with a telephone by his bed and was ready, at any hour of the day or night, to answer an appeal for help. Often he would rise from his bed and drive across the city to bring a blood donor to the sick person's bedside, and often it was he himself who gave the blood that saved a sinking soul.

How often he turned despair into hope, or tears into joy I cannot tell—but from these humble beginnings grew the first blood transfusion service in Scotland, and when he died in 1949, his work covered the whole country.

There are many ways of loving your neighbour, but who can deny that John Copland's was one of the most blessed of all ?

YOU may be sorry that you spoke,
Sorry you stayed or went ;
Sorry you lost or won—perhaps
Sorry so much was spent.
But, as you go through life, you'll find
You're never sorry you were kind.

THE FRIENDSHIP BOOK

HAVING visited one of our larger hospitals, the specialist hurried to his car, and found he had a flat tyre. The hour was late. He had twenty miles to go. He couldn't think of any handy garage that would be open. Somebody must change the wheel.

Well, the hall porter did, but with his fumbling, by a movement of his foot he pushed four of the five nuts of the wheel into a drain—and the surgeon was indeed in a jam.

It was at that moment that the boy looking on, solved the problem. " No need to worry," said he. " You have one nut left of the five. Just take one nut out of each of the other three wheels, and if you drive carefully you can get home with four nuts a wheel instead of five."

What bothered the medical man was why a boy of 12 could think up something he couldn't.

AN old lady and her minister sat talking by the light of the fire. The old widow suddenly said something her minister won't readily forget. " You know," she said, " a bad conscience is really a good conscience !"

At first the minister was taken aback—then he saw, of course, what she meant. It was simply this— if you've even the tiniest scrap of a conscience, it's bound to prick you, for not one of us is perfect. So, if you've a bad conscience there's hope for you —at least it's working !

But if you've a clear conscience all the time—if, day after day, you sail along secure in the belief you have nothing to be ashamed of or sorry for— then God help you, my friend, for you have no conscience at all.

THE FRIENDSHIP BOOK

JUST a thought, borrowed from the baker's man, who called the other day, rubbed his hands, grinned at the Lady of the House, and remarked: " It must be nice to be so comfortably off that you can talk about the pleasures of being poor ! "

And away he went, whistling, before the Lady of the House could say anything.

O LORD, Thou art my God ; I will exalt Thee, I will praise Thy name.

HERE'S to the gallant knitting · needles of New Zealand.

In case you're mystified, let me put you in the picture. Any day now the postie will walk up the path to the Red House Boys' Home in Musselburgh with a big, bulky parcel in his arms. In it will be 30 warm sweaters and a mass of socks and gloves !

The woollens will come from a town near Wellington, just as they have come for almost 20 years. It all began when a homely Scots mother told her friends in New Zealand about the laddies of Red House.

So she and her neighbours bought wool straight from the sheep farm, spun it on their spinning wheels and knitted it into warm clothes for the boys of Musselburgh. When the old lady died, the work she started was carried on in her memory and it has gone on ever since.

It's a fine tribute to the warmth of a woman's heart that it can be touched by the plight of a homeless laddie 12,000 miles away !

TUESDAY—DECEMBER 13.

FRANKLY, there wasn't much that could be said in favour of young John Newton.

His mother, a gentle soul, whom he loved dearly, died when he was seven, and when he was only 11, his father, a ship's captain, took him off to sea with him.

Later, while still in his teens, John was press-ganged into the Royal Navy—and when he attempted to desert, he was flogged for his pains. Then he entered the slave trade and worked in a plantation on the Gold Coast of Africa, indifferent to all the horror and misery around him.

Yet, the strange thing is that when John died at 82, he was a beloved minister—for at 40 he turned aside from his past life and became a country parson. It is well for us that he did, for in our hymn-book there are no fewer than nine hymns by him, among them "Approach, My Soul, the Mercy Seat," "Glorious Things of Thee are Spoken" and perhaps the loveliest of them all—

How sweet the name of Jesus sounds
    In a believer's ear ;
It soothes his sorrows, heals his wounds,
    And drives away his fear . . .

John died serving the faith he had fought so long to destroy—and, through his hymns, he serves it still.

WEDNESDAY—DECEMBER 14.

WHEN winter brings the frost and snow,
    And aches and pains galore,
And draughts that freeze and do not please,
    And troubles by the score,
Smile if you can, since you are not
    The only one who isn't hot

THURSDAY—DECEMBER 15.

DO you know the old story about a Persian king who sent his eldest son on a journey to see a mango tree in winter, his second son to see it in springtime, his third son in summer and his youngest son in autumn. When all four were together in the palace each was asked to describe a mango tree.

" It's an ugly stump," said the eldest.

" It is a thing of beauty, covered with lacy green," said the second.

" Not even the rose has more beautiful blossoms," said the third.

" My elders do not know what they are talking about," said the youngest. " It is a tree filled with pear-like fruits."

" All of which," commented their father, " shows that you must see a mango tree for a year at least before knowing what it is like—and that you need to know a lot about things and people before making conclusions about them."

FRIDAY—DECEMBER 16.

PEGGY'S such a kindly woman, really—you would hardly have expected that she gives her mother, who lives alone, nothing at all for Christmas, apart from a few toffees and a book.

Nothing tangible, that is.

What she does give her mother is a whole day's help—having got the family off her hands before nine in the morning, away goes Peggy in her old skirt and blouse. And how she works when she gets to her mother's ! A sort of December spring clean, if you like ; and, before she leaves, the house is shining—and she and Mum put the decorations up and make no end of mince pies !

Nice Christmas present, really !

THE FRIENDSHIP BOOK

HAVE you seen the wayside pulpit outside a church saying—Be Square All The Week But Come Round On Sunday ?

And have you heard about the girl who, when she was asked if she had enjoyed a party, replied—" It was smashing—a really posh do with a running buffalo !"

HE that despiseth his neighbour sinneth : but he that hath mercy on the poor, happy is he.

MRS MARY SHEARER lives in the village of Montgarrie, in Aberdeenshire. The village is eleven miles from the nearest hospital, and in winter the roads are often blocked.

That is why, nearly 25 years ago, the district nurse knocked at Mrs Shearer's door to ask her if she would look after a young woman who was expecting a baby, for there was a chance the woman's home might be cut off when the baby arrived.

Well, Mrs Shearer was delighted to help—and a few days later the baby was born in her home. Although she didn't know it then, it was the first of many—for her home became the unofficial hospital for mothers-to-be in the district, and 30 babies were brought into the world there.

The first baby is now a bobby. Another is a banker and a third a doctor.

Mrs Shearer's a widow now and lives alone. But she will never forget the many children she helped to bring into the world—and what a joy it is when, as often happens, they drop in to see her.

TUESDAY—DECEMBER 20.

I LISTENED to a service broadcast from the little Highland church of Urquhart, near Drumnadrochit.

The sermon was not preached by the minister—but by a farmer, who's an elder of the church.

It was a fine sermon, full of the understanding and quiet wisdom of a man who lives close to nature. Indeed, I was so impressed that I rang up the minister at Urquhart to compliment him on the service.

And what do you think he told me? He has five other elders in his small congregation who, at a moment's notice, can—and do—preach as fine a sermon as you'd hear from many a minister. What's more, you'd be wrong if you imagined them to be professors, or teachers, or men accustomed to speaking in public.

Two are farmers, one is a forester, another works for the county council, and all speak simply and directly as men who are not afraid to stand up and declare their beliefs.

It strikes me, you know, that this story is a bit of a challenge to you and me, as well as to every elder —and I can't help wondering what we'd think if someone asked us to preach a sermon that was to be broadcast tomorrow!

WEDNESDAY—DECEMBER 21.

*H*OW *very nice it is for me, at Christmas, to recall*
   The thrill my Christmas pennies gave when I was very small.
And now, grown old, it gives me joy when I am in the street,
In memory of Christmas past, to give some child a treat!

THURSDAY—DECEMBER 22.

I CAME across this odd statement the other day—"Religion takes folk in peculiar ways. It sent Mrs Purdy out to buy a new scrubbing brush."

I pondered that. Who Mrs Purdy was I don't know, but what she did is, I think, important. For it serves to remind you and me that, after all, religion really has little to do with being pious or saying long prayers or singing in the choir.

Stripped of all pretence and distortions, religion is essentially living a bit better today than you did yesterday—and that means, in practice, doing your best all along the line, making things sweeter and cleaner, helping anybody, being cheery and friendly . . . trusting that if you put your life in God's hands you needn't worry, because HE will see you through.

FRIDAY—DECEMBER 23.

THIS is the story of a boy who got into trouble a few days before Christmas because he had lost his handkerchief.

His mother had given him a clean hanky on Saturday morning. He had gone out shopping, and came home without it. She was cross. She said he was careless.

The boy's eyes filled with tears. He explained that he simply could not help it. There was nothing else he could do.

On the way home from the shops he had noticed the door of the church open, and had gone inside. He had stood by the crib. He had looked at the figure of the Baby Jesus—and had noticed that there was no pillow for the Holy Child's head.

"What else could I do, Mummy?" he asked. "I just folded my hanky, and said, 'There, Baby Jesus—that will be more comfy'."

SATURDAY—DECEMBER 24.

HOW would you like on Christmas Day to start peeling the biggest pile of potatoes you've ever seen? Or, for that matter, how would you face the job of cleaning hundredweights of vegetables—or washing and drying stacks of dirty dishes?

Well, I know of 40 folk who do just that—not only on Christmas Day, but on Christmas Eve, Hogmanay and New Year's Day, and they do it because of their downright neighbourliness.

They're members of the Edinburgh Jewish Community and they willingly undertake this task every year to allow the kitchen staff of the Royal Infirmary to spend more time with their families during Christmas and New Year.

In these days, when the merits of this faith and that are being argued, a friendly gesture like this seems to me to go right to the roots of the matter—and who can doubt that these fine folk carry the very spirit of Christmas in their hearts?

SUNDAY—DECEMBER 25.

GLORY to God in the highest, and on earth peace, good will towards men.

MONDAY—DECEMBER 26.

TEN-SECOND sermons for a quiet moment:

A wise man will make more opportunities than he finds.

Friendship redoubleth joys, and cutteth griefs in halves.

One can value a house to the last penny, but none can value a home.

Let yesterday be a lesson, today an action, tomorrow a hope.

TUESDAY—DECEMBER 27.

GRANNY lives with her married daughter and her grand-daughter, Elspeth, aged eight, who is, alas, anything but bright at arithmetic.

So every evening after tea Daddy and Elspeth have a session together—an attempt to give the little lady a grounding in sums. It is hard work and there might be a hint of rebellion if it were not for the fact that she cannot have a game with Granny unless Daddy says she really has tried hard.

And Elspeth likes playing draughts with Granny because she always wins!

Bless you, don't begin telling me that Granny contrives to lose . . . let us say it is just a coincidence that Elspeth always wins!

WEDNESDAY—DECEMBER 28.

RING out the old, ring in the new,
We've said it oft before.
We have so many things to do,
The year has much in store.

But first, let's give a word of thanks
For the year now nearly dead ;
And pray that we may walk in peace
Through the days that lie ahead.

THURSDAY—DECEMBER 29.

A WHIMSICAL friend stopped me on the pavement, and remarked, " Is there anything worse than getting up on a dark, cold morning?"

" I cannot imagine anything," I assured him.

He nodded gravely. Then, with a chuckle, he said, " You are right, Francis. But, oh, how wonderful you feel when you've finished thinking about getting up, and you really *are* out of bed !"

FRIDAY—DECEMBER 30.

DO you switch on the radio or TV to get the weather forecast ? Or do you tap the barometer? The Lady of the House does neither.

Observe her making a morning cup of coffee ... a cupful of milk in a pan, the pan on the stove. Watch her scatter a spoonful of coffee on the warm milk, stirring it in.

Up pop the bubbles. This is the exciting moment, for according to a friend :

> *If the bubbles collect in the centre of the pan— fine weather.*
>
> *If the bubbles make a ring round the side—rain.*
>
> *If the bubbles spread out anyhow— changeable weather.*

To me—a mere man—it all sounds like mumbo jumbo, but the Lady of the House (with a twinkle in her eye), says it's infallible ... sometimes !

SATURDAY—DECEMBER 31.

ONE year. Twelve months. Fifty-two weeks. Three hundred and sixty-five days. No matter how you look at it, it's a long time. And, yet, has it really been long enough to do all the things we should have done and meant to do and would have done if only we hadn't been so busy.?

But now we have a new year ahead of us. One year in which to live a better life. Twelve months to spend helping our neighbours. Fifty-two weeks in which to make new friends and to cement old friendships. Three hundred and sixty-five days to pray for a better world.

With God's help, we can do it.

The Lady of the House and I wish you all a very happy New Year.

Where the Photographs were taken

ENCHANTMENT — Bamburgh Castle, Northumberland.

AS WE SHOULD BE . . . — Perth-Inverness Road, Dunkeld,
Perthshire.

THE CARVER — Glen Torridon, Ross and Cromarty.

THE PEACE OF THE HILLS — In the Cairngorms.

WINTER — Glen Lyon, Perthshire.

THINKING IT OUT — Aberdeen.

" MY HOME " — Castlebay, Isle of Barra.

THE BONUS — Shrivenham, Berks.

*SEA LORE — Donegal, Ireland.

THE PATH — Shere, Surrey.

THE PATTERN — Hill of Barra, Aberdeenshire.

QUIET MOMENTS — St Paul's Churchyard, London.

THE LORDLY ONES — Loch Stack, Sutherland.

" IN MEMORIAM " — Pentre Ifan, near Newport,
Pembrokeshire.

FAITH — Buchanty, Perthshire.

THE BAY — Oban, Argyll.

" AWAY FROM IT ALL " — Glen Isla, Angus.

THE VOICES FALL SILENT — Kirk o' Shotts, Lanarkshire.

*By courtesy of the Irish Tourist Association.

Printed and Published by D. C. Thomson & Co., Ltd.
12 Fetter Lane, Fleet Street, London, E.C.4.
© D. C. Thomson & Co., Ltd., 1965.